THIRD EDITION

2A

Skills for Success

LISTENING AND SPEAKING

Margaret Brooks

OXFORD

UNIVERSITY PRESS

OXFORD
UNIVERSITY PRESS

198 Madison Avenue
New York, NY 10016 USA

Great Clarendon Street, Oxford, OX2 6DP, United Kingdom

Oxford University Press is a department of the University of Oxford.
It furthers the University's objective of excellence in research, scholarship,
and education by publishing worldwide. Oxford is a registered trade
mark of Oxford University Press in the UK and in certain other countries

First published in 2020
2024 2023 2022 2021 2020
10 9 8 7 6 5 4 3 2

ISBN: 978 0 19 490490 2   STUDENT BOOK 2A WITH IQ ONLINE PACK
ISBN: 978 0 19 490478 0   STUDENT BOOK 2A AS PACK COMPONENT
ISBN: 978 0 19 490538 1   IQ ONLINE STUDENT WEBSITE

Printed in China

This book is printed on paper from certified and well-managed sources

ACKNOWLEDGMENTS

Back cover photograph: Oxford University Press building/David Fisher
Illustration by: p. 26 Karen Minor

*The Publishers would like to thank the following for their kind permission to
reproduce photographs and other copyright material:* **123RF:** pp. 44 (log
house/Benoit Daoust), (Gaudi house/Aliaksandr Mazurkevich), 50 (road
rage/Antonio Diaz), 89 (friends interacting during meal/Mark Bowden),
141 (yurt/Gilad Fiskus), 154 (coastline/bloodua); **Alamy:** pp. 12 (bookshop
café/Luis Dafos), 13 (booksigning/Jeff Morgan 08), 16 (wearing same
shoes/Glasshouse Images), 18 (cyclist in city traffic/Scott Hortop Travel),
28 (cryptic frog/Dave and Sigrun Tollerton), 33 (colourful building/
Maria Galan), 34 (house in Asir/ERIC LAFFORGUE), 37 (white living
room/Jodie Johnson), 38 (red fire truck/imageBROKER), 52 (crowded
bus/Torontonian), 58 (adults talking on balcony/Hero Images Inc.),
62 (Franklin Roosevelt/From Original Negative), (John Kennedy/Trinity
Mirror /Mirrorpix), 76 (interacting with digital assistant/Image navi –
QxQ images), 77 (GPS in car/age fotostock), 79 (1920s miners cottages/
Allan Cash Picture Library), 93 (two sets of identical twins/Image Source
Plus), 94 (male identical twins/Esther Moreno), 98 (multigenerational
family/Kirn Vintage Stock), 116 (adult playing video game/ZUMA Press,
Inc.), 123 (chess trophy/Kirn Vintage Stock), 146 (nomad family/Lucy
Calder), 162 (irrigation sprinklers/Mauritius images GmbH), 165 (children
carrying water/Jake Lyell), 168 (washing hands/Cultura Creative (RF)),
169 (indoor play area/Piotr Adamowicz), 171 (stomachache/Panther Media
GmbH); **Getty:** pp. cover (Green color tile pattern/Fabian Krause/EyeEm),
4 (pet rocks/Al Freni), 5 (foot boats/Keystone/Stringer), 6 (old lightbulb/
Science & Society Picture Library), 9 (organic vegetables/DOUGBERRY),
11 (bookshop/whitemay), 14 (Kente fabric weaving/Education Images),
23 (young women shopping/Peter Cade), 24 (chameleon/Juan Buitrago),
31 (bowerbird/Education Images), 37 (colourful living room/irina88w),
46 (helping elderly woman/SolStock), 48 (work colleagues heated
discussion/praetorianphoto), 56 (attentive student classroom/skynesher),
67 (family meal/Ken Seet/Corbis/VCG), 68 (playing board games/Hero
Images Inc.), 71 (man on laptop/supersizer), 75 (Tanja Hollander/Portland
Press Herald), 83 (woman looking sad/EXTREME-PHOTOGRAPHER), 90
(large family photo/Amrish Saini/EyeEm), 96 (female twins/serts), 105
(looking at photographic memories/Yevgen Timashov), 107 (mother
and daughter with photo album/RapidEye), 111 (grandmother greeting
daughter/Ariel Skelley), 112 (girls playing video game/DaniloAndjus),
117 (father and son playing video game/Tom Werner), 118 (improve
coordination/Jgalione), 120 (children chess tournament/Hero Images),
121 (Students Play Chess/VCG/Contributor), 124 (chess tournament/
VCG), 128 (game developers/AFP), 136 (family playing cricket/uniquely
india), 137 (family playing card game/shapecharge), 138 (cottage in
mountains/Pete Rowbottom), 149 (modern apartment/pawel. gaul), 155
(Bosco Verticale building/marcociannarel), 157 (television interview/vm),
159 (cave dwellings/Alex Lapuerta), 160 (street cleaner/by MedioTuerto),
169 (outdoor play area/Susanne Kronholm), 176 (shipwrecked man/Martin
Barraud), 178 (cattle drinking from stream/Damian Davies), 183 (woman
cleaning house/Tony Hutchings); **Newscom:** p. 34 (Luis Barragán home/
Javier Lira/Notimex); **OUP:** pp. 70 (woman at telegraph/Shutterstock/
Everett Collection), 99 (DNA/Shutterstock /zffoto), 121–122 (chess pieces/
Shutterstock/Nilotic); **Shutterstock:** pp. 2 (queue for Apple store/
Sascha Steinbach/EPA-EFE/Shutterstock), 7 (velocipede/Imfoto), (fidget
spinner/Olga V Kulakova), 19 (frustrated businessman/Creativa Images),
27 (cat/osobystist), 28 (false leaf katydid/PeingjaiChiangmai), (poison
dart frog/Brandon Alms), 30 (monarch butterfly/Kate Scott), (zebras/
The Maberhood), (coral snake/Mark_Kostich), (arctic fox in summer/
COULANGES), (arctic fox in winter/JoannaPerchaluk), 40 (red jacket/
Neamov), (red shoes/Chiyacat), 44 (modern city apartment/Trong Nguyen),
(trailer home/Lowphoto), 51 (radio interview/antoniodiaz), 55 (disruptive
students/Proshkin Aleksandr), 72 (woman using social media/Rawpixel.
com), 86 (man gesturing confused/PicMy), 92 (left family portrait/
Monkey Business Images), (right family portrait/Asia Images Group), 108
(two people talking/yurakrasil), 114 (Monopoly board/enchanted_fairy),
115 (Scrabble/Wachiwit), 118 (reduce stress/Aquarius Studio), (use as a
learning tool/Rawpixel.com), (practice skills/Gorodenkoff), 125 (students
on computers/mofaez), 126 (Simcity game/Pe3k), (phone screen/Stanisic
Vladimir), 127 (adults playing board game/Standret), 130 (adults playing
charades/Syda Productions), 132 (bowling/Corepics VOF), 133 (hide and
seek/Iakov Filimonov), 140 (goats/Travel Pass Photos), 142 (wolf/Alexandr
Kucheryavko), 143 (nomad herding livestock/CW Pix), 147 (high rise
apartments/Naeblys), 149 (woman looking out of window/shurkin_son),
156 (person in Antarctica/Marcelo Alex), 158 (futuristic settlement on
mars/ustas7777777), 164 (dry river bed/Peter Turner Photography),
170 (hand sanitizer/Elizaveta Galitckaia), 171 (cold/aslysun), 180 (water
depth gauges/prajit48), 181 (wall sanitizer/Alexander Oganezov);
Third party: p. 114 (Landlord's game/Thomas E Forsyth).

ACKNOWLEDGMENTS

We would like to acknowledge the teachers from all over the world who participated in the development process and review of *Q: Skills for Success* Third Edition.

USA

Kate Austin, Avila University, MO; **Sydney Bassett**, Auburn Global University, AL; **Michael Beamer**, USC, CA; **Renae Betten**, CBU, CA; **Pepper Boyer**, Auburn Global University, AL; **Marina Broeder**, Mission College, CA; **Thomas Brynmore**, Auburn Global University, AL; **Britta Burton**, Mission College, CA; **Kathleen Castello**, Mission College, CA; **Teresa Cheung**, North Shore Community College, MA; **Shantall Colebrooke**, Auburn Global University, AL; **Kyle Cooper**, Troy University, AL; **Elizabeth Cox**, Auburn Global University, AL; **Ashley Ekers**, Auburn Global University, AL; **Rhonda Farley**, Los Rios Community College, CA; **Marcus Frame**, Troy University, AL; **Lora Glaser**, Mission College, CA; **Hala Hamka**, Henry Ford College, MI; **Shelley A. Harrington**, Henry Ford College, MI; **Barrett J. Heusch**, Troy University, AL; **Beth Hill**, St. Charles Community College, MO; **Patty Jones**, Troy University, AL; **Tom Justice**, North Shore Community College, MA; **Robert Klein**, Troy University, AL; **Patrick Maestas**, Auburn Global University, AL; **Elizabeth Merchant**, Auburn Global University, AL; **Rosemary Miketa**, Henry Ford College, MI; **Myo Myint**, Mission College, CA; **Lance Noe**, Troy University, AL; **Irene Pannatier**, Auburn Global University, AL; **Annie Percy**, Troy University, AL; **Erin Robinson**, Troy University, AL; **Juliane Rosner**, Mission College, CA; **Mary Stevens**, North Shore Community College, MA; **Pamela Stewart**, Henry Ford College, MI; **Karen Tucker**, Georgia Tech, GA; **Loreley Wheeler**, North Shore Community College, MA; **Amanda Wilcox**, Auburn Global University, AL; **Heike Williams**, Auburn Global University, AL

Canada

Angelika Brunel, Collège Ahuntsic, QC; **David Butler**, English Language Institute, BC; **Paul Edwards**, Kwantlen Polytechnic University, BC; **Cody Hawver**, University of British Columbia, BC; **Olivera Jovovic**, Kwantlen Polytechnic University, BC; **Tami Moffatt**, University of British Columbia, BC; **Dana Pynn**, Vancouver Island University, BC

Latin America

Georgette Barreda, SENATI, Peru; **Claudia Cecilia Díaz Romero**, Colegio América, Mexico; **Jeferson Ferro**, Uninter, Brazil; **Mayda Hernández**, English Center, Mexico; **Jose Ixtaccihuatl**, Instituto Tecnológico de Tecomatlán, Mexico; **Andreas Paulus Pabst**, CBA Idiomas, Brazil; **Amanda Carla Pas**, Instituição de Ensino Santa Izildinha, Brazil; **Allen Quesada Pacheco**, University of Costa Rica, Costa Rica; **Rolando Sánchez**, Escuela Normal de Tecámac, Mexico; **Luis Vasquez**, CESNO, Mexico

Asia

Asami Atsuko, Jissen Women's University, Japan; **Rene Bouchard**, Chinzei Keiai Gakuen, Japan; **Francis Brannen**, Sangmyung University, South Korea; **Haeyun Cho**, Sogang University, South Korea; **Daniel Craig**, Sangmyung University, South Korea; **Thomas Cuming**, Royal Melbourne Institute of Technology, Vietnam; **Nguyen Duc Dat**, OISP, Vietnam; **Wayne Devitte**, Tokai University, Japan; **James D. Dunn**, Tokai University, Japan; **Fergus Hann**, Tokai University, Japan; **Michael Hood**, Nihon University College of Commerce, Japan; **Hideyuki Kashimoto**, Shijonawate High School, Japan; **David Kennedy**, Nihon University, Japan; **Anna Youngna Kim**, Sogang University, South Korea; **Jae Phil Kim**, Sogang University, South Korea; **Jaganathan Krishnasamy**, GB Academy, Malaysia; **Peter Laver**, Incheon National University, South Korea; **Hung Hoang Le**, Ho Chi Minh City University of Technology, Vietnam; **Hyon Sook Lee**, Sogang University, South Korea; **Ji-seon Lee**, Iruda English Institute, South Korea; **Joo Young Lee**, Sogang University, South Korea; **Phung Tu Luc**, Ho Chi Minh City University of Technology, Vietnam; **Richard Mansbridge**, Hoa Sen University, Vietnam; **Kahoko Matsumoto**, Tokai University, Japan; **Elizabeth May**, Sangmyung University, South Korea; **Naoyuki Naganuma**, Tokai University, Japan; **Hiroko Nishikage**, Taisho University, Japan; **Yongjun Park**, Sangji University, South Korea; **Paul Rogers**, Dongguk University, South Korea; **Scott Schafer**, Inha University, South Korea; **Michael Schvaudner**, Tokai University, Japan; **Brendan Smith**, RMIT University, School of Languages and English, Vietnam; **Peter Snashall**, Huachiew Chalermprakiet University, Thailand; **Makoto Takeda**, Sendai Third Senior High School, Japan; **Peter Talley**, Mahidol University, Faculty of ICT, Thailand; **Byron Thigpen**, Sogang University, South Korea; **Junko Yamaai**, Tokai University, Japan; **Junji Yamada**, Taisho University, Japan; **Sayoko Yamashita**, Jissen Women's University, Japan; **Masami Yukimori**, Taisho University, Japan

Middle East and North Africa

Sajjad Ahmad, Taibah University, Saudi Arabia; **Basma Alansari**, Taibah University, Saudi Arabia; **Marwa Al-ashqar**, Taibah University, Saudi Arabia; **Dr. Rashid Al-Khawaldeh**, Taibah University, Saudi Arabia; **Mohamed Almohamed**, Taibah University, Saudi Arabia; **Dr Musaad Alrahaili**, Taibah University, Saudi Arabia; **Hala Al Sammar**, Kuwait University, Kuwait; **Ahmed Alshammari**, Taibah University, Saudi Arabia; **Ahmed Alshamy**, Taibah University, Saudi Arabia; **Doniazad sultan AlShraideh**, Taibah University, Saudi Arabia; **Sahar Amer**, Taibah University, Saudi Arabia; **Nabeela Azam**, Taibah University, Saudi Arabia; **Hassan Bashir**, Edex, Saudi Arabia; **Rachel Batchilder**, College of the North Atlantic, Qatar; **Nicole Cuddie**, Community College of Qatar, Qatar; **Mahdi Duris**, King Saud University, Saudi Arabia; **Ahmed Ege**, Institute of Public Administration, Saudi Arabia; **Magda Fadle**, Victoria College, Egypt; **Mohammed Hassan**, Taibah University, Saudi Arabia; **Tom Hodgson**, Community College of Qatar, Qatar; **Ayub Agbar Khan**, Taibah University, Saudi Arabia; **Cynthia Le Joncour**, Taibah University, Saudi Arabia; **Ruari Alexander MacLeod**, Community College of Qatar, Qatar; **Nasir Mahmood**, Taibah University, Saudi Arabia; **Duria Salih Mahmoud**, Taibah University, Saudi Arabia; **Ameera McKoy**, Taibah University, Saudi Arabia; **Chaker Mhamdi**, Buraimi University College, Oman; **Baraa Shiekh Mohamed**, Community College of Qatar, Qatar; **Abdulcelah Mohammed**, Taibah University, Saudi Arabia; **Shumaila Nasir**, Taibah University, Saudi Arabia; **Kevin Onwordi**, Taibah University, Saudi Arabia; **Dr. Navid Rahmani**, Community College of Qatar, Qatar; **Dr. Sabah Salman Sabbah**, Community College of Qatar, Qatar; **Salih**, Taibah University, Saudi Arabia; **Verna Santos-Nafrada**, King Saud University, Saudi Arabia; **Gamal Abdelfattah Shehata**, Taibah University, Saudi Arabia; **Ron Stefan**, Institute of Public Administration, Saudi Arabia; **Dr. Saad Torki**, Imam Abdulrahman Bin Faisal University, Dammam, Saudi Arabia; **Silvia Yafai**, Applied Technology High School/Secondary Technical School, UAE; **Mahmood Zar**, Taibah University, Saudi Arabia; **Thouraya Zheni**, Taibah University, Saudi Arabia

Turkey

Sema Babacan, Istanbul Medipol University; **Bilge Çöllüoğlu Yakar**, Bilkent University; **Liana Corniel**, Koc University; **Savas Geylanioglu**, Izmir Bahcesehir Science and Technology College; **Öznur Güler**, Giresun University; **Selen Bilginer Halefoğlu**, Maltepe University; **Ahmet Konukoğlu**, Hasan Kalyoncu University; **Mehmet Salih Yoğun**, Gaziantep Hasan Kalyoncu University; **Fatih Yücel**, Beykent University

Europe

Amina Al Hashamia, University of Exeter, UK; **Irina Gerasimova**, Saint-Petersburg Mining University, Russia; **Jodi**, Las Dominicas, Spain; **Marina Khanykova**, School 179, Russia; **Oksana Postnikova**, Lingua Practica, Russia; **Nina Vasilchenko**, Soho-Bridge Language School, Russia

CRITICAL THINKING

The unique critical thinking approach of the *Q: Skills for Success* series has been further enhanced in the Third Edition. New features help you analyze, synthesize, and develop your ideas.

Unit question

The thought-provoking unit questions engage you with the topic and provide a critical thinking framework for the unit.

 UNIT QUESTION

How can colors be useful?

A. Discuss these questions with your classmates.

1. Why can wearing dark clothes at night be dangerous? Why do traffic police in some countries wear orange?

2. Imagine you want to paint your house. What color do you choose? Why?

3. Look at the photo. How is color useful to this animal?

Analysis

You can discuss your opinion of each listening text and analyze how it changes your perspective on the unit question.

 SAY WHAT YOU THINK

SYNTHESIZE Think about the unit video, Listening 1, and Listening 2 as you discuss the questions.

1. Many families in the world today have family members who live in different countries. How does this affect family life? What are the advantages and disadvantages?

2. How important is it to keep in touch with your larger family, that is aunts, uncles, cousins, grandparents, and so on?

3. Who has been an important person in your life? It might be a family member or other person. Why is the person important?

NEW! Critical Thinking Strategy with video

Each unit includes a Critical Thinking Strategy with activities to give you step-by-step guidance in critical analysis of texts. An accompanying instructional video (available on iQ Online) provides extra support and examples.

NEW! Bloom's Taxonomy

Pink activity headings integrate verbs from Bloom's Taxonomy to help you see how each activity develops critical thinking skills.

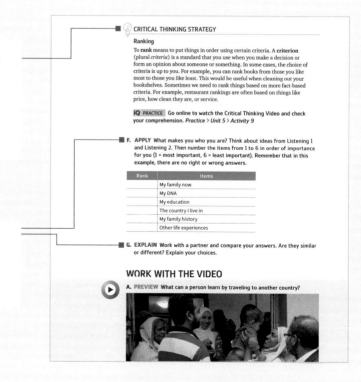

CRITICAL THINKING STRATEGY

Ranking

To **rank** means to put things in order using certain criteria. A **criterion** (plural *criteria*) is a standard that you use when you make a decision or form an opinion about someone or something. In some cases, the choice of criteria is up to you. For example, you can rank books from those you like most to those you like least. This would be useful when cleaning out your bookshelves. Sometimes we need to rank things based on more fact-based criteria. For example, restaurant rankings are often based on things like price, how clean they are, or service.

iQ PRACTICE Go online to watch the Critical Thinking Video and check your comprehension. *Practice > Unit 5 > Activity 9*

F. APPLY What makes you who you are? Think about ideas from Listening 1 and Listening 2. Then number the items from 1 to 6 in order of importance for you (1 = most important, 6 = least important). Remember that in this example, there are no right or wrong answers.

Rank	Items
	My family now
	My DNA
	My education
	The country I live in
	My family history
	Other life experiences

G. EXPLAIN Work with a partner and compare your answers. Are they similar or different? Explain your choices.

WORK WITH THE VIDEO

A. PREVIEW What can a person learn by traveling to another country?

THREE TYPES OF VIDEO

UNIT VIDEO

The unit videos include high-interest documentaries and reports on a wide variety of subjects, all linked to the unit topic and question.

NEW! "Work with the Video" pages guide you in watching, understanding, and discussing the unit videos. The activities help you see the connection to the Unit Question and the other texts in the unit.

NEW! In some units, one of the main listening texts is a video.

CRITICAL THINKING VIDEO

NEW! Narrated by the *Q* series authors, these short videos give you further instruction on the Critical Thinking Strategy of each unit using engaging images and graphics. You can use them to gain a deeper understanding of the Critical Thinking Strategy.

SKILLS VIDEO

NEW! These instructional videos provide illustrated explanations of skills and grammar points in the Student Book. They can be viewed in class or assigned for a flipped classroom, for homework, or for review. One skill video is available for every unit.

Easily access all videos in the Resources section of iQ Online.

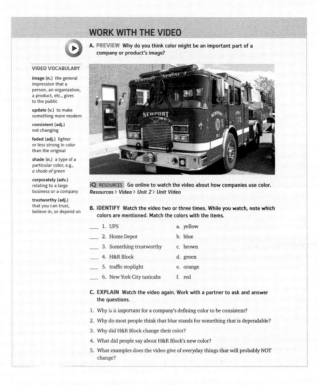

WORK WITH THE VIDEO

A. PREVIEW Why do you think color might be an important part of a company or product's image?

VIDEO VOCABULARY

image (n.) the general impression that a person, an organization, a product, etc., gives to the public

update (v.) to make something more modern

consistent (adj.) not changing

faded (adj.) lighter or less strong in color than the original

shade (n.) a type of a particular color, e.g., *a shade of green*

corporately (adv.) relating to a large business or a company

trustworthy (adj.) that you can trust, believe in, or depend on

iQ RESOURCES Go online to watch the video about how companies use color.
Resources > Video > Unit 2 > Unit Video

B. IDENTIFY Watch the video two or three times. While you watch, note which colors are mentioned. Match the colors with the items.

___ 1. UPS a. yellow
___ 2. Home Depot b. blue
___ 3. Something trustworthy c. brown
___ 4. H&R Block d. green
___ 5. traffic stoplight e. orange
___ 6. New York City taxicabs f. red

C. EXPLAIN Watch the video again. Work with a partner to ask and answer the questions.

1. Why is it important for a company's defining color to be consistent?
2. Why do most people think that blue stands for something that is dependable?
3. Why did H&R Block change their color?
4. What did people say about H&R Block's new color?
5. What examples does the video give of everyday things that will probably NOT change?

How to compare and contrast

Venn Diagram

Firefighter	Both	Police Officer
fights fires	*help people*	*fights crime*
stays at the station until called	*have dangerous jobs*	*works on the street*

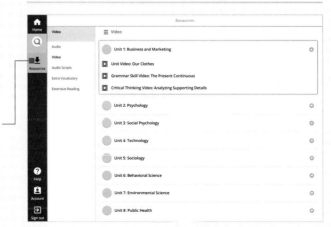

VOCABULARY

A research-based vocabulary program focuses on the words you need to know academically and professionally.

The vocabulary syllabus in *Q: Skills for Success* is correlated to the CEFR (see page 90) and linked to two word lists: the Oxford 3000 and the OPAL (Oxford Phrasal Academic Lexicon).

⚷ OXFORD 3000

The Oxford 3000 lists the core words that every learner at the A1– B2 level needs to know. Items in the word list are selected for their frequency and usefulness from the Oxford English Corpus (a database of over 2 billion words).

Vocabulary Key
In vocabulary activities, ⚷ shows you the word is in the Oxford 3000 and **OPAL** shows you the word or phrase is in the OPAL.

PREVIEW THE LISTENING

A. VOCABULARY Here are some words and phrases from Listening 2. Read the definitions. Then complete each sentence with the correct word or phrase.

attentive *(adjective)* watching or listening carefully
courteous *(adjective)* polite, having courtesy
deal with *(verb phrase)* to solve a problem
improve *(verb)* ⚷ OPAL to make something better
influence *(noun)* ⚷ OPAL the power to change how someone or something acts
principal *(noun)* the person in charge of a school
respect *(noun)* ⚷ OPAL consideration for the rights and feelings of other people
shout out *(verb phrase)* to say something in a loud voice
valuable *(adjective)* ⚷ OPAL very useful or important

⚷ Oxford 3000™ words   **OPAL** Oxford Phrasal Academic Lexicon

1. I apologized to show Sue I have _____ for her feelings.

2. The parents are meeting with the _____ tonight to discuss problems at school. She can make new school rules to stop the problems.

OPAL
OXFORD PHRASAL ACADEMIC LEXICON

NEW! The OPAL is a collection of four word lists that provide an essential guide to the most important words and phrases to know for academic English. The word lists are based on the Oxford Corpus of Academic English and the British Academic Spoken English corpus. The OPAL includes both spoken and written academic English and both individual words and longer phrases.

Academic Language tips in the Student Book give information about how words and phrases from the OPAL are used and offer help with features such as collocations and phrases.

ACADEMIC LANGUAGE
The word *relationship* is often used in academic contexts. Notice that the suffix *-ship* is also used in the noun *friendship*. The suffix *-ship* indicates a state or condition.

| OPAL
Oxford Phrasal Academic Lexicon

3. We need curtains on those windows. Without them, we have no _____ in the bedroom.

4. It is hard to discuss some things online. You need a _____ conversation where you can see the other person.

5. His _____ with Tom is very important to Reza. They have known each other for many years.

6. The newspaper _____ said that there will be bad snowstorms in the Midwest today.

7. Their family has lived here _____. I mean a very long time, more than 100 years.

8. The lecturer made some very _____ statements about social media. It gave me a lot to think about.

iQ PRACTICE Go online for more practice with the vocabulary.
Practice > Unit 4 > Activities 3–4

B. PREVIEW You are going to listen to a lecture about social media and friendship. Work with a partner. List one good thing and one possible problem related to social media and friendships.

WORK WITH THE LISTENING

🔊 **A. LISTEN AND TAKE NOTES** Listen to Part 1 of the lecture. The speaker mentions three points that will be in the lecture. Prepare a piece of paper to take notes. List the three points and leave space for writing after each one.

EXTENSIVE READING

NEW! Extensive Reading is a program of reading for pleasure at a level that matches your language ability.

There are many benefits to Extensive Reading:

- It helps you to become a better reader in general.
- It helps to increase your reading speed.
- It can improve your reading comprehension.
- It increases your vocabulary range.
- It can help you improve your grammar and writing skills.
- It's great for motivation to read something that is interesting for its own sake.

Each unit of *Q: Skills for Success* Third Edition has been aligned to an Oxford Graded Reader based on the appropriate topic and level of language proficiency. The first chapter of each recommended graded reader can be downloaded from iQ Online Resources.

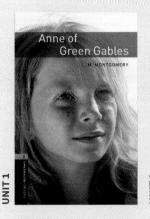

UNIT 1

UNIT 2

UNIT 3

UNIT 4

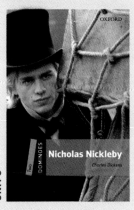

UNIT 5

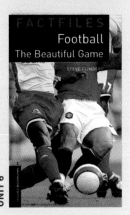

UNIT 6

UNIT 7

UNIT 8

iQ ONLINE extends your learning beyond the classroom.

- Practice activities provide essential skills practice and support.
- Automatic grading and progress reports show you what you have mastered and where you need more practice.
- The Discussion Board allows you to discuss the Unit Questions and helps you develop your critical thinking.
- Essential resources such as audio and video are easy to access anytime.

NEW TO THE THIRD EDITION

- iQ Online is optimized for mobile use so you can use it on your phone.
- An updated interface allows easy navigation around the activities, tests, resources, and scores.
- New Critical Thinking Videos expand on the Critical Thinking Strategies in the Student Book.
- The Extensive Reading program helps you improve your vocabulary and reading skills.

How to use iQ ONLINE

Go to **Practice** to find additional practice and support to complement your learning in the classroom.

Go to **Resources** to find:
- All Student Book video
- All Student Book audio
- Critical Thinking videos
- Skills videos
- Extensive Reading

Go to **Messages** and **Discussion Board** to communicate with your teacher and classmates.

Online tests assigned by your teacher help you assess your progress and see where you need more practice.

A progress bar shows you how many activities you have completed.

View your scores for all activities.

AUTHOR AND CONSULTANTS

AUTHOR

Margaret Brooks worked for many years as a teacher and administrator in a variety of English language-teaching programs in the Dominican Republic and Costa Rica, including serving as a professor at the Autonomous University of Santo Domingo and working with a private company to develop specialized language courses for businesses in Costa Rica. She has also written and developed course material for a wide range of ELT programs.

SERIES CONSULTANTS

Lawrence J. Zwier holds an M.A. in TESL from the University of Minnesota. He is currently the Associate Director for Curriculum Development at the English Language Center at Michigan State University in East Lansing. He has taught ESL/EFL in the United States, Saudi Arabia, Malaysia, Japan, and Singapore.

Marguerite Ann Snow holds a Ph.D. in Applied Linguistics from UCLA. She teaches in the TESOL M.A. program in the Charter College of Education at California State University, Los Angeles. She was a Fulbright scholar in Hong Kong and Cyprus. In 2006, she received the President's Distinguished Professor award at CSULA. She has trained ESL teachers in the United States and EFL teachers in more than 25 countries. She is the author/editor of numerous publications in the areas of content-based instruction, English for academic purposes, and standards for English teaching and learning. She is a co-editor of *Teaching English as a Second or Foreign Language* (4th ed.).

CRITICAL THINKING CONSULTANT **James Dunn** is a Junior Associate Professor at Tokai University and the Coordinator of the JALT Critical Thinking Special Interest Group. His research interests include critical thinking skills' impact on student brain function during English learning as measured by EEG. His educational goals are to help students understand that they are capable of more than they might think and to expand their cultural competence with critical thinking and higher-order thinking skills.

ASSESSMENT CONSULTANT **Elaine Boyd** has worked in assessment for over 30 years for international testing organizations. She has designed and delivered courses in assessment literacy and is also the author of several EL exam coursebooks for leading publishers. She is an Associate Tutor (M.A. TESOL/Linguistics) at University College, London. Her research interests are classroom assessment, issues in managing feedback, and intercultural competences.

VOCABULARY CONSULTANT **Cheryl Boyd Zimmerman** is Professor Emeritus at California State University, Fullerton. She specialized in second-language vocabulary acquisition, an area in which she is widely published. She taught graduate courses on second-language acquisition, culture, vocabulary, and the fundamentals of TESOL, and has been a frequent invited speaker on topics related to vocabulary teaching and learning. She is the author of *Word Knowledge: A Vocabulary Teacher's Handbook* and Series Director of *Inside Reading, Inside Writing*, and *Inside Listening and Speaking*, published by Oxford University Press.

ONLINE INTEGRATION **Chantal Hemmi** holds an Ed.D. TEFL and is a Japan-based teacher trainer and curriculum designer. Since leaving her position as Academic Director of the British Council in Tokyo, she has been teaching at the Center for Language Education and Research at Sophia University in an EAP/CLIL program offered for undergraduates. She delivers lectures and teacher trainings throughout Japan, Indonesia, and Malaysia.

COMMUNICATIVE GRAMMAR CONSULTANT **Nancy Schoenfeld** holds an M.A. in TESOL from Biola University in La Mirada, California, and has been an English language instructor since 2000. She has taught ESL in California and Hawaii and EFL in Thailand and Kuwait. She has also trained teachers in the United States and Indonesia. Her interests include teaching vocabulary, extensive reading, and student motivation. She is currently an English Language Instructor at Kuwait University.

CONTENTS

Business and Marketing

 UNIT QUESTION

How important is it to keep up with current trends?

A. Discuss these questions with your classmates.

1. What are some of the latest trends in your community? Think about things like clothing, food, and technology.

2. How do these trends affect the way people live, use technology, or shop?

3. Look at the photo. Why are these people waiting in line?

B. Listen to *The Q Classroom* online. Then answer these questions.

1. How important does Sophy think it is to keep up with the latest changes in technology?

2. Do Marcus and Yuna agree with Sophy? Why or why not?

3. How is Felix's response different from that of the others?

iQ PRACTICE Go to the online discussion board to discuss the Unit Question with your classmates. *Practice > Unit 1 > Activity 1*

UNIT OBJECTIVE

Listen to a podcast and a conversation. Gather information and ideas to create a survey about trends.

3

When you take notes, write only *key* words—the most important words. Don't spend time writing little words like *of*, *the*, *and*, etc. Here are some ways to identify key words as you listen:

- Listen for repeated words. These often point to the main idea.

- Focus on words that the speaker defines. If a speaker takes time to say what a word means, it's probably important.

- Listen for words the speaker emphasizes by saying them more slowly or a little louder.

A. IDENTIFY Read the beginning of a lecture about the difference between a trend and a fad. Underline words that you think are important. The word *fad* is underlined as an example.

To be successful in business, it is important to be able to tell the difference between a <u>fad</u> and a trend. A fad is something that becomes popular quite suddenly but does not last very long. A trend is the general direction in which something is developing or growing. In business, following a trend usually leads to more success than chasing after a fad. Trying to make money on a fad is risky.

B. APPLY Listen as the speaker continues the lecture. Identify important words as you hear them and take notes. Does the speaker repeat any of the words you underlined in Activity A?

C. DISCUSS Compare notes with a partner. Which words did you underline? Why?

iQ PRACTICE Go online for more practice identifying key words while taking notes. *Practice › Unit 1 › Activity 2*

LISTENING 1

OBJECTIVE ▶

They Said It Was Just a Fad

You are going to listen to a podcast about inventions that some people thought were just fads. As you listen, gather information and ideas about the importance of keeping up with current trends.

PREVIEW THE LISTENING

A. VOCABULARY Here are some words from Listening 1. Read the sentences. Then match each underlined word with its definition on page 6.

____ 1. That popular restaurant chain has to make a lot of money. The person who started it must be very <u>wealthy</u> now.

____ 2. During the winter months here, it is <u>essential</u> to have a warm coat. It gets very cold!

____ 3. I need to get the <u>brakes</u> on my car fixed. I'm having problems stopping.

____ 4. Sales of the toys went up in November and December, but they <u>declined</u> in January.

____ 5. Our attempt to build a robot was a complete <u>failure</u>. It just didn't work at all.

____ 6. My daughter loves that song that says, "The <u>wheels</u> on the bus go round and round." I'm tired of hearing it!

____ 7. They live in an <u>enormous</u> house. It has six bedrooms.

____ 8. Now, that car is way too expensive, but this smaller one is quite <u>affordable</u>.

ACADEMIC LANGUAGE

The verb *decline* is common in spoken and written academic English. It is often used with adverbs that describe the degree of the decline: for example, *decline significantly | slowly | rapidly*.

_____|**OPAL**
Oxford Phrasal Academic Lexicon

a. *(adjective)* completely necessary

b. *(verb)* to become smaller, fewer, or less

c. *(noun)* a person or thing that is unsuccessful

d. *(adjective)* having a lot of money and property

e. *(noun)* round objects under a car or other vehicle that turn when it moves

f. *(adjective)* not expensive; cheap enough for most people to be able to buy

g. *(noun)* the parts of a car or other vehicle that make it go slower or stop

h. *(adjective)* very large

iQ PRACTICE Go online for more practice with the vocabulary.
Practice > Unit 1 > Activities 3–4

B. PREVIEW You are going to listen to a podcast called *They Said It Was Just a Fad*. It describes three inventions that people thought were just fads and would never be used to create a successful business. Work with a partner. What key words do you think you will hear? Make a list.

WORK WITH THE LISTENING

A. LISTEN AND TAKE NOTES Listen to the podcast. Write any key words you hear. Leave space on the page to add more notes later. Here are some words to get you started.

Lightbulb

    Edison

    affordable

    change lives

Bicycle

Fidget spinner

B. EXTEND Listen again. Add more information to your notes.

C. ANALYZE Check (✓) the two statements that express the main ideas in the podcast.

_____ 1. Some things that people thought were just fads became successful businesses in the end.

_____ 2. A business based on a fad, like fidget spinners, will always lose money.

_____ 3. It sometimes takes a long time before you know if something will last or if it is just a fad.

 D. EXPLAIN Answer the questions. Then listen and check your answers.

TIP FOR SUCCESS

Many students are nervous about listening. Take a deep breath and relax! If you are nervous or stressed, it's more difficult to listen and understand what you hear.

1. What did J. P. Morgan do to show that he believed in Edison's lightbulbs?

_____

2. What did Morgan's father think about the idea of having electric light?

_____

3. Why were the early bicycles called *velocipedes* dangerous to ride?

_____

4. How were "safety" bicycles different from velocipedes?

_____

5. Did bicycle use decline after more people had cars?

_____

6. Why have bicycles been a successful area of business for so many years?

_____

7. What is a fidget spinner, and what is it used for?

_____

8. Does the speaker say whether the spinners are a fad or a lasting trend? Why or why not?

_____

E. IDENTIFY Which invention does each comment below apply to? Mark each as *L* (lightbulb), *B* (bicycle), or *F* (fidget spinner).

____ 1. One inventor thought making it affordable would change people's lives.

____ 2. This trend "is ending and you missed it!"

____ 3. A scientist described it as a complete failure.

____ 4. Now "only the rich will burn candles."

____ 5. In 1902, one newspaper said that as a fad, the activity was dead.

____ 6. They "are not just a fad" because they help people deal with stressful situations.

F. CATEGORIZE Read the words and phrases in the word box. Write the words associated with each item in the appropriate column of the chart.

~~affordable~~	brakes	candles	cheap electricity
fuel	nervous energy	play around	transportation
triangular toy	wheels		

Lightbulb	Bicycle	Fidget spinner
affordable		

iQ PRACTICE Go online for additional listening and comprehension.
Practice › Unit 1 › Activity 5

SAY WHAT YOU THINK

DISCUSS Discuss the questions in a small group.

1. Think of a fad that is no longer popular, such as pet rocks. How long did it last? Why did it die out?

2. What is something that is newly popular in your community now? Is it a fad or a trend? Why?

3. A friend of yours wants to start a business selling robot fish as "pets." These are mechanical fish. You put them in water and they "swim" around. Will this be a fad or a trend? Will it be successful? Explain.

The **main idea** is the most important thing the speaker wants you to understand. Speakers often use several strategies to emphasize their main idea. Listen for repeated words and ideas. Listen for emphasis on certain words or sentences. Also listen for speakers to summarize the main ideas at the end of their talk.

A. ANALYZE Listen to a report from a panel discussion about the future of food. Check (✓) the sentence that best states the main idea of the report.

____ 1. In the future, the food industry needs to be entirely focused on vegetarian choices.

____ 2. People say they want healthier foods, but in fact they buy a lot of foods that aren't good for them.

____ 3. The movement toward having healthier foods with clear labels will continue.

B. INTERPRET Look at these words from the listening.

1. Are there any you did not hear or understand? Circle them.

available	bother	brand	cuisine
evident	entrepreneur	fertilizer	grocery
hummus	transparency		

2. Why was it possible to understand the main idea without knowing all of these words?

3. What words or ideas did the speaker repeat or emphasize? How did they help you understand the main idea?

iQ PRACTICE Go online for more practice listening for main ideas.
Practice > Unit 1 > Activity 6

 **CRITICAL THINKING STRATEGY**

Analyzing supporting details

It is important to analyze the details and examples that a speaker uses to support his or her main ideas. If an idea is not supported well, listeners will think the idea has no value. Ask: *Does this example support the main idea?* In some cases, the answer might be that it doesn't. Look at these examples.

Main idea: The trend toward healthier foods is going to continue.

Example: Shoppers spend a lot every year on sodas and sweet treats.

This example doesn't support the main idea. In fact, it says the opposite. The speaker uses it to present another side of the issue.

Main idea: The bicycle was a fad that became a trend.

Example: Today, people in cities all around the world use bicycles for transportation.

This example supports the main idea by showing that bicycles continue to be popular.

iQ PRACTICE Go online to watch the Critical Thinking Video and check your comprehension. *Practice > Unit 1 > Activity 7*

C. ANALYZE Choose the example that <u>best</u> supports each main idea.

1. Sometimes hard work and a strong belief can make an invention successful.

   a. Today, many things we use every day depend on electricity.

   b. J. P. Morgan's father thought that Edison's ideas wouldn't work and that electricity was just a fad.

   c. Edison believed that electricity would change lives, so he installed 400 lightbulbs in Morgan's home.

2. It's too soon to tell whether the fidget spinner is a fad or a trend.

   a. The popularity of other inventions often increased and decreased over time.

   b. With the spinner, people can fidget in boring meetings and not disturb others.

   c. Many people think spinners help people reduce stress levels.

3. A successful bookstore has to be more than just a place to buy books.

   a. Children's bookstores continue to be successful.

   b. Corner Store Books invited the local chess club to meet at the store.

   c. There are fewer shoppers downtown these days because so many stores are closing.

D. EXPLAIN Work with a partner. Compare your answers in Activity A and explain your choices.

LISTENING 2　Bucking the Trend

OBJECTIVE ▶

You are going to listen to a conversation between two friends, Asha and Kim. Asha wants to open a new business. As you listen, gather information and ideas about the importance of keeping up with current trends.

PREVIEW THE LISTENING

A. VOCABULARY Here are some words and phrases from Listening 2. Read the definitions. Then complete each sentence with the correct word or phrase.

> **advertise** *(verb)* 🔑 to publish information to persuade people to buy
> something
>
> **buck the trend** *(verb phrase)* to do something that goes against what is
> currently popular or fashionable
>
> **chat** *(verb)* 🔑 to talk to someone in a friendly, informal way
>
> **get the point** *(verb phrase)* to understand the main idea of something
>
> **postage** *(noun)* the amount of money it costs to send a letter, package, etc.
>
> **potential** *(adjective)* 🔑 OPAL that may possibly become something
>
> **realize** *(verb)* 🔑 to come to understand that something is true
>
> **reasonable** *(adjective)* 🔑 OPAL not too expensive

🔑 Oxford 3000™ words　　　　　　　　　OPAL Oxford Phrasal Academic Lexicon

1. I'm sorry I don't have time to _____ right now. Let's talk later, I have to leave for an appointment.

2. They want $5,000 for their car. I think that's a _____ price.

3. He talked for an hour, but I still didn't _____. What was he trying to say?

4. What's the _____ to mail a letter to Canada?

5. If you want your store to be successful, you have to _____. If you don't, no one will know it's here.

6. They're interviewing two _____ candidates for the job. Jay thinks either of them will work well with our team.

7. Jack always tries to _____. He wants to be different from everyone else.

8. I didn't _____ that e-books were so popular! I'm happy to learn that.

iQ PRACTICE Go online for more practice with the vocabulary.
Practice > Unit 1 > Activities 8–9

B. PREVIEW You're going to listen to *Bucking the Trend,* a conversation between two people, Asha and Kim. Asha wants to buy and run a bookstore, like some other stores that are "bucking the trend." Kim thinks it may be risky. What problems could there be with this plan? Discuss with a partner.

WORK WITH THE LISTENING

 A. LISTEN AND TAKE NOTES Listen to the conversation. First, prepare a note page with two columns labeled *Pro* and *Con. Pro* is for arguments that support starting a bookstore business. *Con* is for arguments against it. As you listen, write key words in each column. Leave space to add to your notes later.

Pro	Con
independent small	risky

 B. EXTEND Listen again. Add more information to your notes.

C. EVALUATE Compare notes with a partner. Correct and edit your notes as needed.

D. IDENTIFY Read the questions. Choose the correct answers.

1. Which of these is NOT a reason Asha gives for wanting to open a bookstore?

   a. She likes to read print books instead of e-books.

   b. She wants to work for herself, not for other people.

   c. She saw a bookstore for sale nearby at a good price.

2. Why does Kim think Asha's plan might be risky?

   a. Fewer people are reading books now.

   b. Bookstores are gathering places for people in the community.

   c. People nowadays are buying more books online, not in stores.

3. What has Asha's research shown her?

   a. She should open a store just for children's books.

   b. Small, independent bookstores can be successful.

   c. People are now buying more e-books than print books.

4. What does Kim like about shopping in bookstores?

   a. Stores are less crowded than they used to be.

   b. She can buy a book and take it home right away.

   c. She doesn't have to talk to people while she's shopping.

E. EXPLAIN Work with a partner. The graph below shows the percentage of book purchases that were e-books from 2012 to 2016. Answer the questions.

1. Which category had the highest percentage of e-book sales in all five years? Why do you think this is so?

2. Which category had the lowest percentage of e-book sales? How can you explain this?

3. How do nonfiction e-book sales compare to fiction e-book sales?

4. How can you describe the trend toward e-book sales between 2012 and 2016?

5. Do these statistics support Asha's idea that she can "buck the trend" toward e-books and open a bookstore? Why or why not?

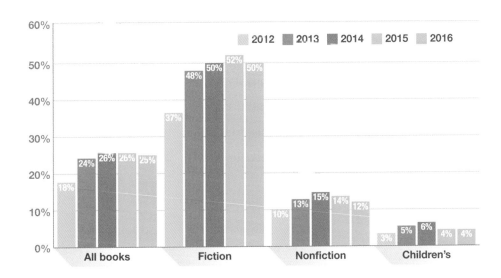

WORK WITH THE VIDEO

A. PREVIEW What do you do with clothes that you can't or don't want to wear anymore? Do you prefer traditional clothing or modern clothing?

VIDEO VOCABULARY

secondhand (adj.)
not new; already used or owned by somebody else

give away (v.)
to give something to someone without asking for or receiving money in return

historian (n.)
a person who is an expert in history

traditional (adj.)
following older methods or ideas rather than modern ones

kente (n.) a handmade cloth from Ghana, famous for its bright colors and original designs

iQ RESOURCES Go online to watch the video about trends in clothing in Ghana. *Resources › Video › Unit 1 › Unit Video*

B. INTERPRET Choose the correct answers.

1. Where does most of the clothing in the market come from?

   a. Africa

   b. China

   c. Europe

2. What does the woman say about the piece of clothing she is looking at?

   a. It's too expensive.

   b. It's the best quality.

   c. It's in bad condition.

3. What does the historian say about traditional clothing?

   a. In the past, people used traditional clothing to tell the history of the country.

   b. It's cheaper than secondhand clothing from Europe and America.

   c. People will always want to wear traditional clothing.

4. What does the woman in the city say about traditional and European clothing?

    a. Traditional clothing was popular a couple of years ago, but it isn't popular now.

    b. Traditional clothing is now "cooler," more popular, than European clothing.

    c. She prefers to wear European clothing when she goes out.

C. EXPLAIN Watch the video again. Discuss the questions in a small group.

1. Why do you think traditional clothing is more expensive than secondhand clothing in Ghana?

2. Is it important for countries to keep their traditional clothing styles? Why or why not?

SAY WHAT YOU THINK

SYNTHESIZE Think about the unit video, Listening 1, and Listening 2 as you discuss the questions.

1. How do you feel about buying secondhand clothing? What other things do people sometimes buy secondhand?

2. Like traditional Ghanaian clothing, some things go out of style for a time and then come back. What things can you think of that were out of style for a time but are popular now?

3. Describe a time in your life when you decided to "buck a trend"—that is, do something your own way, not following what others were doing. Was it a successful experience? Why or why not?

VOCABULARY SKILL Collocations: nouns and verbs

Collocations are groups of words that are commonly used together. One type of collocation is the combination of a **verb** + **noun**.

The word web shows verbs often used with the noun *risk*.

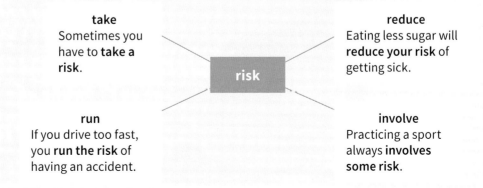

take
Sometimes you have to **take a risk**.

reduce
Eating less sugar will **reduce your risk** of getting sick.

risk

run
If you drive too fast, you **run the risk** of having an accident.

involve
Practicing a sport always **involves some risk**.

TIP FOR SUCCESS
Look at the words around a word you don't know. They can help you find the meaning of the new word.

A. IDENTIFY Read the sentences. Underline each verb used as a collocation with the noun *trend*.

1. Hey, your shoes look cool! I'm going to get some, too. We can start a trend.

2. Franco doesn't like to follow architectural trends. His buildings follow a classical style.

3. I wasn't trying to set a new trend in transportation. I ride my bike to work because the bus schedule doesn't work for me.

4. More and more people are driving cars, even for short distances. I want to buck this trend and start walking everywhere I go.

5. Buildings in my city are getting more energy efficient. I hope architects continue this trend.

B. APPLY Complete the word web. Use the words you underlined in Activity A.

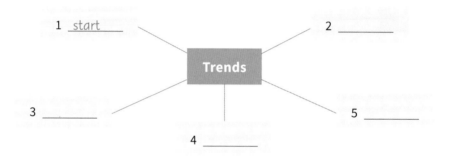

1 _start_   2 _____

                        Trends

3 _____   5 _____

                    4 _____

iQ PRACTICE Go online for more practice using noun-verb collocations.
Practice > Unit 1 > Activity 10

SPEAKING

OBJECTIVE ▶

At the end of this unit, you are going to work in a group to do some "trend spotting" and then present your findings to the class. As you speak, you will need to highlight your main ideas.

GRAMMAR The present continuous

We use the **present continuous** to describe actions taking place at the moment of speaking. Look at this example from Listening 2. It describes what Asha is doing at that moment.

> **Kim:** What are you doing?
> **Asha:** I'm calling the agent for the store.

We can also use the present continuous to describe actions taking place around but not exactly at the moment of speaking. These actions continue for a period of time. Look at this sentence from Listening 2. It describes a trend that is continuing into the future.

> Statistics show that people **are still buying** more print books than e-books.

How to form the present continuous:

Affirmative

Use a form of *be* + verb + *-ing*

> She **is buying** a book now.

Negative

Use the word *not* before the *-ing* verb (*be* + *not* + verb + *-ing*).

> He **is not using** his car to go to work this week.

iQ RESOURCES Go online to watch the Grammar Skill Video.
Resources ⟩ Video ⟩ Unit 1 ⟩ Grammar Skill Video

A. COMPOSE Write sentences with the present continuous. Then read your sentences to a partner.

1. Sales / independent bookstores / increase / all the time

   _____

2. Everyone / wear / red these days / because it's a trendy color!

   _____

3. We / discuss / the difference / between a fad and a trend

_____

4. More people / ride / bicycles / to work these days

_____

 **B. ANALYZE** Listen to the conversations. Decide whether each describes actions that are happening now or actions that are happening around now. Check (✓) the correct answer.

	Happening now	Happening around now
1.	☐	☐
2.	☐	☐
3.	☐	☐
4.	☐	☐
5.	☐	☐
6.	☐	☐

iQ PRACTICE Go online for more practice with the present continuous. *Practice > Unit 1 > Activity 11*

iQ PRACTICE Go online for the Grammar Expansion: present continuous and simple present. *Practice > Unit 1 > Activity 12*

Interjections are short words, phrases, or sounds that people use when they speak. Interjections often express feelings. For example, *Wow!* is an interjection that usually indicates surprise or excitement.

Wow! That was a quick decision.

The meaning of an interjection often depends on the speaker's **intonation**. For example, *Oh!* can express different emotions, as in these examples.

Oh! Look at all the customers coming into the store! (happiness)

Oh! Our sales declined again this month. (disappointment)

Oh! Someone parked in front of the driveway. Now we can't get into the garage! (anger)

Sometimes speakers use an interjection just to give themselves time to think. Sounds like *hmm* and *uh* are used in this way.

Hmm. I know what you mean.

EVALUATE Listen to the sentences. The same speaker will read each one twice with different intonation. Answer the questions. Check (✓) the correct answer.

1. Well, I think this is the right answer.

   Which sentence sounds less sure?

   ___ 1   ___ 2

2. Yeah, and after we finish this project, we're going to do another one.

   Which sentence sounds more excited?

   ___ 1   ___ 2

3. Yeah, I lost my presentation.

   Which sentence sounds more disappointed?

   ___ 1   ___ 2

4. Oh! Mr. Lombardi is going to be in Tokyo next week.

   Which sentence sounds happier?

   ___ 1   ___ 2

iQ PRACTICE Go online for more practice with interjections and intonation.
Practice > Unit 1 > Activity 13

SPEAKING SKILL Drawing attention to main ideas

When you speak, help listeners understand your main ideas.

- Repeat an important idea with different words.

  Morgan's father thought electric light was just a fad. **In other words**, he thought it wouldn't last.

- Use phrases for emphasis.

  The point is that many people *enjoy* going to bookstores.

- Summarize the main ideas of the presentation.

  To sum up, it isn't always easy to start something completely new.

A. DISCUSS Work in a small group. Choose one of the following statements and discuss it for one minute. Give examples and draw attention to the main ideas. Take turns.

1. [Your own idea] is just a fad. It will never last.

2. Electricity was one of the most important discoveries of all time.

3. Twenty years from now there will be more (or no more) bookstores.

B. DISCUSS Listen to the other members of your group. Note the expressions that people use as they give examples and draw attention to their main idea. Discuss your notes with the group.

iQ PRACTICE Go online for more practice with drawing attention to main ideas. *Practice > Unit 1 > Activity 14*

UNIT ASSIGNMENT An experiment with trend spotting

OBJECTIVE ▶

In this section, you are going to work with a small group to conduct an experiment with "trend spotting." You will conduct a survey using your classmates as your subjects and then present your findings to the class. As you prepare your presentation, think about the Unit Question, "How important is it to keep up with current trends?" Use information from Listening 1, Listening 2, the unit video, and your work in this unit to support your presentation. Refer to the Self-Assessment checklist on page 22.

CONSIDER THE IDEAS

 INVESTIGATE Listen to Uma and Dareen's discussion about trend spotting. Answer the questions.

1. What is trend spotting?

2. What is one example of a way in which people use trend spotting?

3. What is a survey?

4. How does Uma feel about the focus on trends? Do you agree? Explain.

PREPARE AND SPEAK

A. GATHER IDEAS Work with a small group. Prepare your trend spotting experiment.

1. Choose a subject from the list below or use your own idea.

Trends in:
• Clothing
• Food
• Technology
• Books
• Transportation

2. Prepare a survey question or questions for your classmates about the topic you have chosen.

3. Conduct the survey. Talk to your classmates and take notes about their answers.

B. ORGANIZE IDEAS With your group, discuss the answers you receive and plan your presentation.

1. Summarize the responses to your survey in a chart.

2. Plan the presentation, making sure each person has a role to play. What were the results of the survey? If you were a business person, how could you use this information? How did you feel about the activity?

C. SPEAK Practice your presentation. Then give your presentation to the class or in a small group. Refer to the Self-Assessment checklist below before you begin.

iQ PRACTICE Go online for your alternate Unit Assignment.
Practice › Unit 1 › Activity 15

CHECK AND REFLECT

A. CHECK Think about the Unit Assignment as you complete the Self-Assessment checklist.

SELF-ASSESSMENT	Yes	No
I was able to speak easily about the topic.	☐	☐
My group or class understood me.	☐	☐
I used the present continuous correctly.	☐	☐
I used vocabulary from the unit.	☐	☐
I drew attention to the main ideas.	☐	☐
I used intonation to express feelings.	☐	☐
I analyzed supporting details.	☐	☐

B. REFLECT Discuss these questions with a partner or group.

1. What is something new you learned in this unit?

2. Look back at the Unit Question—How important is it to keep up with current trends? Is your answer different now than when you started this unit? If yes, how is it different? Why?

iQ PRACTICE Go to the online discussion board to discuss the questions.
Practice › Unit 1 › Activity 16

TRACK YOUR SUCCESS

IQ PRACTICE Go online to check the words and phrases you have learned in this unit. *Practice › Unit 1 › Activity 17*

Check (✓) the skills and strategies you learned. If you need more work on a skill, refer to the page(s) in parentheses.

NOTE-TAKING	☐ I can identify key words. (p. 4)
LISTENING	☐ I can listen for main ideas. (p. 9)
CRITICAL THINKING	☐ I can analyze supporting details. (p. 10)
VOCABULARY	☐ I can recognize and use noun and verb collocations. (p. 15)
GRAMMAR	☐ I can use the present continuous. (p. 17)
PRONUNCIATION	☐ I can use interjections and intonation. (p. 19)
SPEAKING	☐ I can draw attention to main ideas. (p. 20)

OBJECTIVE ▶ ☐ I can gather information and ideas to make a presentation about a current trend.

2 Psychology

 UNIT QUESTION

How can colors be useful?

A. Discuss these questions with your classmates.

1. Why can wearing dark clothes at night be dangerous? Why do traffic police in some countries wear orange?

2. Imagine you want to paint your house. What color do you choose? Why?

3. Look at the photo. How is color useful to this animal?

B. Listen to *The Q Classroom* online. Then match the ideas in the box to the students in the chart.

a. to affect moods	e. different-colored notebooks
b. for symbolic reasons	f. to organize
c. hospitals use relaxing colors	g. wearing school colors
d. to attract attention	h. big red letters on a sign

	Use of color	Example
Sophy	b. for symbolic reasons	
Felix		
Marcus		
Yuna		

iQ PRACTICE Go to the online discussion board to discuss the Unit Question with your classmates. *Practice › Unit 2 › Activity 1*

Listen to a nature program and a panel presentation. Gather information and ideas to give a presentation about the uses of color.

Instructors often use visual elements in their classes. They sometimes refer to pictures in a textbook or show photographs and charts on a screen. They also draw simple pictures and diagrams on the board. To use a visual element in your notes, you can . . .

- first copy the picture or diagram into your notes.

- then label the picture and write notes around it.

You don't need to be a great artist to use pictures in your notes. Even a rough drawing will help you remember the contents of the class.

A. **IDENTIFY** Look at the picture of a leaf used in a biology class and read the instructor's explanation. Then finish labeling the student's drawing and write notes.

The Structure of a Leaf

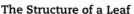
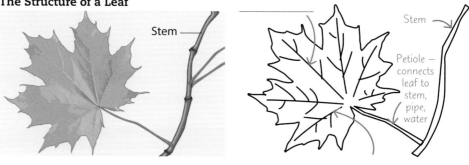

The leaves are the food-making part of a plant. The *petiole* connects the leaf to a *stem* on the plant. The petiole is like a small tube or pipe. It carries water and minerals to the leaf. Water goes from the petiole to the *midrib*. The midrib runs from the bottom to the top of the leaf. Then small *veins* distribute this water all through the leaf. The petiole also turns the leaf toward the sun. This is important because leaves use energy from the sun to make food from carbon dioxide in the air and water. This process is called *photosynthesis*.

B. **APPLY** Look at the picture of the tree. Make a drawing of it. Then listen as an instructor describes the parts of a tree and make notes.

iQ PRACTICE Go online for more practice using visual elements in your notes. *Practice > Unit 2 > Activity 2*

Parts of a tree

LISTENING

The Colors of Nature

You are going to listen to part of a nature program. A famous scientist talks about how animals use color. As you listen, gather information and ideas about how colors can be useful.

PREVIEW THE LISTENING

A. VOCABULARY Here are some words from Listening 1. Read the sentences. Then choose the answer that best matches the meaning of each underlined word.

1. Animals <u>hide</u> when danger is near. They come out when it's safe.
   a. go to a place where no one can see them
   b. come out and look around

2. Listen to that bird. I think it's giving the other birds a <u>warning</u> that there's a cat hunting them.
   a. a call that means hunger
   b. a call that means danger

3. Don't let the children touch that. It is rat <u>poison</u>. It can hurt them.
   a. something that is dangerous to touch or eat
   b. something that has a very bad taste

4. This hand cream makes your <u>skin</u> soft and beautiful.

   a. outer covering of your body

   b. shoes and clothing

5. Some large birds have <u>wings</u> that are more than six feet across.

   a. body parts used to walk

   b. body parts used to fly

6. Most pets can't <u>survive</u> in the wild. They need people to take care of them.

   a. stay alive

   b. find friends

7. Lions are <u>predators</u>. Other animals stay away from lions because they are dangerous.

   a. animals that live in a group

   b. animals that kill and eat other animals

8. All <u>insects</u> have six legs, and many have wings. Most are very small.

   a. an animal like an ant or a bee

   b. an animal like a cat or a rabbit

iQ PRACTICE Go online for more practice with the vocabulary.
Practice > Unit 2 > Activities 3–4

B. PREVIEW **You are going to listen to a nature program about ways animals use color. Work with a partner. Discuss these questions.**

1. Look at photos 1 and 2. Why is it difficult to see the animals in these photos?

2. Look at photo 3. Is it easy or difficult to see the frog?

3. Why do you think the animals have these colors?

A false-leaf katydid

A cryptic frog

A blue poison dart frog

WORK WITH THE LISTENING

A. INVESTIGATE Look at the photos again. Make rough sketches of the animals on a page for your notes. Label the photos and make notes about what you see—for example, color, size, or location. Leave room on the page to add more information.

B. LISTEN AND TAKE NOTES Listen to the nature program and take more notes about each animal in the photos.

C. CATEGORIZE Complete the chart with the words in the box. Then listen and check your answers.

| among the green leaves | blue | brown |
| on the forest floor | green | in the rain forest |

	False-leaf katydid	Cryptic frog	Poison dart frog
Color			
Location			

D. IDENTIFY Read the sentences. Then listen again. Choose the answer that best completes each statement.

1. The false-leaf katydid's ____ look just like leaves.

   a. eyes   b. wings   c. legs

2. The katydid gets its name from ____.

   a. a girl named Katy   b. the way it looks   c. a sound it makes

3. The colors of the cryptic frog match the leaves and ____ on the forest floor.

   a. rocks   b. insects   c. flowers

4. The best way to see a cryptic frog is to ____.

   a. wait for the wind to blow   b. watch for it to move   c. look under a rock

5. The blue poison dart frog has enough poison to kill ____.

   a. one person   b. five people   c. ten people

6. Poison dart frogs live in the rain forests of ____.

   a. South America   b. South Africa   c. North America

E. EXPLAIN Work with a partner. Take turns asking and answering the questions. Use your own words.

1. What does the word *camouflage* mean? Why do animals use camouflage?

2. How does the poison dart frog use color? How is it different from the cryptic frog?

F. CATEGORIZE Read the descriptions of these animals. Do you think they use color for camouflage or as a warning? Write *C* (camouflage) or *W* (warning). Compare answers with a partner.

____ 1. Monarch butterflies are bright orange. Their wings have a terrible taste.

____ 2. Zebras are African animals in the horse family. They have black and white stripes. You often find them standing in tall grass.

____ 3. The coral snake lives in forests. It has red, yellow, and black stripes.

____ 4. The arctic fox has brown or gray fur in the summer, but in winter its fur changes to white.

iQ PRACTICE Go online for additional listening and comprehension.
Practice > Unit 2 > Activity 5

SAY WHAT YOU THINK

DISCUSS Discuss the questions in a group.

1. Think about the animals in Activity D on page 29. Do these animals use color for camouflage or as a warning? Explain.

2. Most large predators, like lions, are not brightly colored. Why do you think this is true?

3. What are some ways people use color as camouflage or as a sign of danger?

A **cause** is the action that makes something happen. An **effect** is what happens as a result. In a sentence, the cause can come before the effect or after it.

Connecting words like *so* and *because* show a cause or an effect. Listen for them carefully. *So* shows an effect. *Because* shows a cause.

Pollution was a poison to the frogs, **so** the frogs in the pond died.
cause   effect

The frogs survived **because** their camouflage matched the leaves.
effect   cause

A. IDENTIFY Read and listen to these statements about the nature program you heard in Listening 1. Circle the cause in each statement. Underline the effect.

1. Katydids are hard to see because of their green color.

2. Predators can't see the katydids, so the katydids stay safe.

3. It's hard to see the cryptic frog because it uses camouflage.

4. The cryptic frog is the same color as the leaves, so you can't see it very well.

5. The blue poison dart frog is bright blue, so you can see it easily.

6. Dart frogs are dangerous because their skins contain a strong poison.

B. ANALYZE Listen to the scientist talk about Australian bowerbirds. Then match each cause with the correct effect.

Cause	Effect
___ 1. The satin bowerbird decorates its bower with blue things.	a. The bower looks nice.
___ 2. The bowerbird doesn't like red.	b. Predators cannot find the nest easily.
___ 3. The female builds a nest in a tree.	c. The bowerbird removes the red thing.

iQ PRACTICE Go online for more practice with listening to understand cause and effect. *Practice > Unit 2 > Activity 6*

A male bowerbird and its bower

Evaluating cause-and-effect statements

A cause-and-effect statement makes a connection between two ideas. It says that one thing **caused** the other, which is the **effect**, or result. It is important to think critically about a statement like this. Ask, "Is it true, or valid?" A valid cause-and-effect statement is based on facts or something that is true.

Here is an example of a valid cause-and-effect statement.

> It's dangerous to touch dart frogs because their skin contains a strong poison.

The statement is supported by the fact that scientists have proven that dart frogs are too poisonous even to touch. The cause is the poison, and the effect is that it's dangerous for people to touch dart frogs.

Here is a clearly false cause-and-effect statement.

> It rained today because I washed my car. Every time I wash my car it rains.

There is no real connection between the rain and someone washing his or her car. The fact that two things often occur at the same time does not necessarily mean that one causes the other. There is no valid evidence to support this cause-and-effect statement.

iQ PRACTICE Go online to watch the Critical Thinking Video and check your comprehension. *Practice ⟩ Unit 2 ⟩ Activity 7*

C. ANALYZE Read these statements and decide if they show valid cause-and-effect relationships. Mark each one as *V* (valid) or *N* (not valid). Then write a sentence to explain your answer. Discuss your answers as a class.

1. The frog population declined this summer because there was no rain and it was very hot.

   V—This is probably valid because frogs need water to survive.

2. People say that katydids stop singing when it rains. Yesterday, it rained because the katydids stopped singing.

   _____

3. The bark of trees protects them from insects and weather. That tree died because someone cut all of the bark off it.

   _____

4. The bowerbird removed the stone from his bower because it was red, not blue. We see this again and again. He only puts blue things in his bower.

   _____

5. I just learned that bowerbirds exist, so they must be a newly discovered kind of bird.

   _____

LISTENING 2   Colorful Homes

OBJECTIVE ▶

You are going to listen to a class presentation about two different areas of the world where people enjoy very colorful houses. The presentation includes photographs of the houses. As you listen, gather information and ideas about how colors can be useful.

PREVIEW THE LISTENING

VOCABULARY SKILL REVIEW

In Unit 1, you learned about verb + noun collocations. Look for three or more verb + noun collocations in Activity A and underline them.

A. VOCABULARY Here are some words and phrases from Listening 2. Read the sentences. Then choose the sentence that best matches the meaning of the original sentence.

1. We painted the wall a <u>solid</u> red.

   a. The wall has only one color, red.

   b. The wall has a mix of red and other colors.

2. The flowers in the vase are a <u>brilliant</u> yellow.

   a. The flowers are dark yellow.

   b. The flowers are a very bright yellow.

3. The brown and red colors of the houses <u>blend in</u> with the desert landscape.

   a. The colors of the houses are similar to the colors of the desert.

   b. The colors of the houses are different from the colors of the desert.

4. It is difficult to draw a <u>straight</u> line if you don't have a ruler.

   a. It is hard to draw a line that goes directly from one point to another.

   b. It is hard to draw a perfect circle.

5. The garden is a very <u>peaceful</u> place to sit and relax.

    a. The garden is a noisy place with a lot of activity.

    b. The garden is a very calm and quiet place.

6. The design of the house is based on the <u>shape</u> of a triangle.

    a. The house has the same form as a triangle.

    b. The builder used a tool called a triangle to build the house.

7. The beauty and color of their homes give the women of Asir a sense of <u>pride</u>.

    a. They feel pleased and satisfied with their work.

    b. They can charge a lot for their work because it is good.

8. Look at those white clouds in the bright blue sky. They're really <u>beautiful</u>.

    a. It's probably going to rain soon.

    b. The sky and clouds are very nice to look at.

9. Look, the color of your scarf <u>matches</u> the color of my sweater.

    a. Your scarf and my sweater are the same color.

    b. The color of your scarf is more beautiful than the color of my sweater.

iQ PRACTICE Go online for more practice with the vocabulary.
Practice > Unit 2 > Activities 8–9

B. PREVIEW Look at the two photos from the presentation. How are the colors different? Discuss with a partner.

A Luis Barragán building

A home in Asir, Saudi Arabia

WORK WITH THE LISTENING

🔊 **A. LISTEN AND TAKE NOTES** Listen to Part 1 of the panel presentation about the work of the Mexican architect Luis Barragán. Take notes. Remember to write only the most important words.

🔊 **B. LISTEN AND TAKE NOTES** Listen to Part 2 of the panel presentation about the houses in the province of Asir in Saudi Arabia. Take notes. Remember to write only the most important words.

🔊 **C. APPLY** Complete the summary of the presentations with the words and phrases in the box. Use your notes to help you. Then listen and check your answers.

Part 1:

architecture	bright colors	gardens	peaceful

The presentation was about the use of color in ___architecture___ in
1

two different parts of the world, Mexico and the province of Asir in Saudi

Arabia. In Mexico, the architect Luis Barragán was famous for his use of

_____ in his buildings. The _____ around the
2   3

homes were also important to him. He wanted the homes he built to be beautiful

and _____ places for the people who lived there.
4

Part 2:

artistic	colorful designs	shapes	special tradition	women

The province of Asir in Saudi Arabia has a _____
5

of painting houses with _____ during the festival of Eid.
6

The designs use _____ like triangles and squares in many
7

different colors. The _____ do the painting, and they get a sense
8

of pride from making their homes beautiful. Today people are working to keep

this _____ tradition alive.
9

D. CATEGORIZE Work with a partner. Complete the chart with information about the two topics in the presentation. Then listen again and check your answers.

	Luis Barragán	The women of Asir
Country		
Typical colors		
Special features		

E. IDENTIFY Choose the answer that best completes each statement.

1. Luis Barragán used the colors of ____ in his architecture.

   a. buildings of American small towns

   b. houses in the small towns of Mexico

   c. houses in Mexico City

2. Barragán often painted the walls of his houses ____.

   a. with pictures of brightly colored flowers

   b. with complicated designs

   c. with strong, solid colors

3. Barragán liked the architecture of North Africa because ____.

   a. the houses were painted in bright colors

   b. the buildings blended in with the colors of the desert landscape

   c. the houses were large enough for many people to live in them

4. In the province of Asir, it is a tradition for people to paint their homes ____.

   a. every year

   b. every other year

   c. every five years

5. In the designs, lines going up and down are used to represent ____.

   a. houses

   b. water or lightning

   c. children

6. Competitions encourage modern artists ____.

   a. to create completely new designs for painting the houses

   b. to sell their artwork at fairs

   c. to use traditional designs in their artwork

F. CATEGORIZE Write *T* (true) or *F* (false). Then correct the false statements.

____ 1. For Luis Barragán, the landscape and gardens around a house were not important.

_____

____ 2. Barragán's travels to Europe and North Africa in the 1920s and 1930s had an influence on his architecture.

_____

____ 3. The large triangles in the designs painted on the houses in Asir represent rivers near the home.

_____

____ 4. The moderator of the panel discussion comments that the architectural traditions of Mexico and Saudi Arabia are similar in some ways.

_____

G. DISCUSS Work in a group. Look at the photos of the two living rooms. Which one would you prefer to have in your home? Why?

WORK WITH THE VIDEO

A. PREVIEW Why do you think color might be an important part of a company or product's image?

VIDEO VOCABULARY

image (n.) the general impression that a person, an organization, a product, etc., gives to the public

update (v.) to make something more modern

consistent (adj.) not changing

faded (adj.) lighter or less strong in color than the original

shade (n.) a type of a particular color, e.g., *a shade of green*

corporately (adv.) relating to a large business or a company

trustworthy (adj.) that you can trust, believe in, or depend on

iQ RESOURCES Go online to watch the video about how companies use color.
Resources > Video > Unit 2 > Unit Video

B. IDENTIFY Watch the video two or three times. While you watch, note which colors are mentioned. Match the colors with the items.

____ 1. UPS   a. yellow

____ 2. Home Depot   b. blue

____ 3. Something trustworthy   c. brown

____ 4. H&R Block   d. green

____ 5. traffic stoplight   e. orange

____ 6. New York City taxicabs   f. red

C. EXPLAIN Watch the video again. Work with a partner to ask and answer the questions.

1. Why is it important for a company's defining color to be consistent?

2. Why do most people think that blue stands for something that is dependable?

3. Why did H&R Block change their color?

4. What did people say about H&R Block's new color?

5. What examples does the video give of everyday things that will probably NOT change?

SAY WHAT YOU THINK

SYNTHESIZE Think about the unit video, Listening 1, and Listening 2 as you discuss the questions.

1. How can you compare the way animals use color with the way people use color?

2. Do any companies and businesses in your community use color branding? If so, what colors do they use? Are there any colors that would NOT be good for a company? Explain.

VOCABULARY SKILL Word families: nouns and verbs

Some words can be used as a **noun** or a **verb**. To know if a word is a noun or a verb, you have to look at the words around it.

⌈ There are pictures of the architect's **work** on the Internet. (noun)
⌊ The men **work** at the building site every day. (verb)

A word is probably a noun if it comes after . . .

* an article (*a, an,* or *the*).

* an adjective.

* a number.

* the words *this, that, these,* or *those.*

A word may be a verb if it comes after . . .

* a pronoun such as *it* or *they.*

* a time word such as *sometimes* or *never.*

* a helping verb such as *do, does, can, will,* or *should.*

A. CATEGORIZE Look at the bold word in each sentence. Write *N* (noun) or *V* (verb).

___V___ 1. We can **camouflage** this birdhouse. We can paint it the same color as the tree.

_____ 2. An owl is a bird that flies at night. It calls, "Hoo, hoo, hoo." It **sounds** like it's asking, "Who? Who? Who?"

_____ 3. The **poison** of that insect is very strong, but it can't kill a person.

_____ 4. There are many different **sounds** in the forest at night.

_____ 5. The colors of the insect's wings **blend in** with the leaves.

_____ 6. Both of these shirts are blue, but the colors don't **match**. This one is darker.

_____ 7. The color green is actually a **blend** of blue and yellow.

_____ 8. That liquid is dangerous. It can **poison** people and animals.

ACADEMIC LANGUAGE

The verb *change* is common in spoken and written academic English. It is often used with the prepositions *from* and *to*. In winter, the color of the Arctic fox *changes from brown to* white.

_____ **OPAL**
Oxford Phrasal Academic Lexicon

B. APPLY Complete each sentence with the correct word from the box. Then write *N* (noun) or *V* (verb).

camouflage	change	fight	match	poison	sound

1. When these birds are young, they are brown and white. When they become adults, their colors _____*change*_____ to black and orange.   V

2. When catbirds sing, the _____ is like cats meowing.   ___

3. Bowerbirds sometimes _____ other birds for building materials.   ___

4. They're trying to _____ the buildings by painting them brown and green.   ___

5. Can the skin of the dart frog _____ me if I touch it?   ___

6. Is the red in these shoes a good _____ with the red in my jacket?   ___

iQ PRACTICE   Go online for more practice using word families.
Practice › Unit 2 › Activity 10

SPEAKING

OBJECTIVE ▶

At the end of this unit, you are going to design a house or an apartment building. Make sure to give examples when you describe the building to group members.

GRAMMAR *There's* and *it's*

There's (There is) is used when something is being mentioned for the first time.

> **There's** a <u>bookstore</u> on campus.
>
> **There's** a <u>software program</u> called Camouflage. It hides your files so others can't find them.
>
> **There's** a <u>tree</u> on the roof of that building!

The pronoun *it* in the expression *it's (it is)* refers to something we already know.

> The <u>dart frog</u> is bright blue. Predators know that **it's** dangerous.
>
> I don't like the <u>color</u> of that wall. **It's** too bright.

iQ RESOURCES Go online to watch the Grammar Skill Video.
Resources > Video > Unit 2 > Grammar Skill Video

A. APPLY Complete the paragraph with *there's* and *it's*.

TIP FOR SUCCESS

The pronoun *it* refers to both male and female animals. You can also use the pronouns *he* and *she* for animals when you know the gender of the animal.

There are many different animals in the park. _____There's_____ a
                                                     1
bright red bird in a tree. _____ a male cardinal. Nearby
                                   2
_____ a similar bird, but _____ brown, not red.
         3   4
_____ a female cardinal. On a flower, _____ a
         5   6
beautiful orange and black butterfly. _____ a monarch butterfly.
                                               7
Predators can see it easily. But they also know that _____
                                                               8
a dangerous insect. Its wings have a terrible taste. Its color is a warning to
predators.

B. COMPOSE Work with a partner. Imagine that you are in a place in your city. Describe what you see, using *there's* and *it's*. Take turns.

> A: *There's a little store on that corner. I think it's a shoe store.*
>
> B: *There's a new exhibition at the museum. It's about the first trip to the moon.*

iQ PRACTICE Go online for more practice with *there's* and *it's*.
Practice > Unit 2 > Activities 11–12

The **schwa** sound is the most common vowel sound in English. It is the same sound speakers make when they pause and say *Uh*. It is a very relaxed sound. Unstressed syllables often use the schwa. In dictionaries the pronunciation of the schwa is usually shown with the symbol /ə/.

The word *banana* is a good example of the schwa. The first and last syllables have the schwa. Note that the stressed syllable /næ/ is longer than the other syllables.

/bə ˈnæ nə/

The underlined syllables in these words also use the schwa. These are all unstressed syllables. Remember that any vowel can have the schwa sound.

a-<u>ni</u>-mal   poi-<u>son</u>   <u>sur</u>-vive   pre-<u>da</u>-tor   for-<u>est</u>

The schwa is common in unstressed syllables, but it is sometimes used in stressed syllables.

<u>hun</u>-gry   <u>mo</u>-ney

A. APPLY Listen and write the words. There is one unstressed syllable with the schwa sound in each word. Circle the syllable that contains the schwa sound.

1. camouflage
2. _____
3. _____
4. _____
5. _____
6. _____
7. _____
8. _____

B. IDENTIFY Listen again. Then practice with a partner. Take turns saying the words.

C. EVALUATE Listen to these pairs of words. Which word has the schwa sound in the underlined syllable? Circle your answers.

1. <u>tra</u>dition   <u>tra</u>ffic
2. <u>men</u>tion   ele<u>ment</u>
3. <u>an</u>swer   <u>an</u>other
4. <u>pro</u>gram   <u>pro</u>tection

D. APPLY Work with a partner. Underline all the syllables with the schwa sound. Then take turns reading the sentences.

1. It is a traditional festival that we celebrate every year.

2. Is there an apartment for rent on State Street?

3. We need to find another answer to the problem.

4. There's a special program to protect the city's water.

iQ PRACTICE Go online for more practice with schwa in unstressed syllables.
Practice > Unit 2 > Activity 13

SPEAKING SKILL Asking for and giving examples

When you explain something, give **examples** to help the listener understand your ideas. When you don't understand something a speaker says, ask for an example.

Giving an example:

⌐ For example, . . .
| For instance, . . .
∟ Here's an example.

Asking for an example:

⌐ Can you give me an example?
∟ Do you have any examples?

A. ANALYZE Listen to the excerpts from the Listenings in this unit. How do the speakers introduce or ask for examples? Write the expressions they use.

1. _____

2. _____

3. _____

4. _____

B. PRACTICE Work with a partner. Choose one of the topics below. Tell your partner about the topic. Take turns asking for and giving examples.

- the best colors for the rooms of a house

- why I love the colors of the desert (or the mountains, the beach, etc.)

- my favorite colors to wear

iQ PRACTICE Go online for more practice with asking for and giving examples.
Practice > Unit 2 > Activity 14

UNIT ASSIGNMENT Present a building design

OBJECTIVE ▸

In this section, you are going to present a design of a house or an apartment building. As you prepare your design, think about the Unit Question, "How can colors be useful?" Use information from Listening 1, Listening 2, the unit video, and your work in this unit to support your presentation. Refer to the Self-Assessment checklist on page 45.

1 CONSIDER THE IDEAS

DISCUSS Look at the photos. Then discuss the questions in a group.

1. Which building do you like the most? Why?

2. Which building do you like the least? Why?

3. Do you like buildings that blend into their environments or buildings that are unusual? Explain.

PREPARE AND SPEAK

A. GATHER IDEAS Work in a group. You are going to design a building. Complete the steps.

1. Decide on the type of building. Is it an apartment building or a house?

2. Choose a location for the building. Is your building in a city, a town, or the country? _____ Our building is in a ____.

   a. desert area: dry without many green plants

   b. forest area: green with a lot of trees

   c. large city: downtown with a lot of people and buildings

   d. large city: quiet street near the edge of the city

   e. beach town: near the ocean

B. ORGANIZE IDEAS Discuss with your group what the building looks like from the outside. Then create an outline, using the categories below. Use visual elements in your notes to help show what your building looks like.

- building type
- location
- materials (concrete, wood, glass, metal, etc.)
- outside colors
- plan (how big, how many floors, how many rooms, etc.)
- blends in or is unusual?

C. SPEAK Present your building design to another group. Refer to the Self-Assessment checklist on page 45 before you begin.

1. Use your outline and visual elements from Activity B to help you.

2. Make sure that each person in the group takes part in the presentation.

3. Give examples and show some visual elements to help your audience to better understand.

iQ PRACTICE Go online for your alternate Unit Assignment.
Practice > Unit 2 > Activity 15

CHECK AND REFLECT

A. CHECK Think about the Unit Assignment as you complete the Self-Assessment checklist.

SELF-ASSESSMENT	Yes	No
I used visual elements to show my ideas.	☐	☐
I was able to speak easily about the topic.	☐	☐
My audience understood me.	☐	☐
I used *there's* and *it's*.	☐	☐
I used vocabulary from the unit.	☐	☐
I asked for and gave examples.	☐	☐
I used the schwa in unstressed syllables.	☐	☐

B. REFLECT Discuss these questions with a partner or group.

1. What is something new you learned in this unit?

2. Look back at the Unit Question—How can colors be useful? Is your answer different now than when you started this unit? If yes, how is it different? Why?

iQ PRACTICE Go to the online discussion board to discuss the questions. *Practice > Unit 2 > Activity 16*

TRACK YOUR SUCCESS

iQ PRACTICE Go online to check the words and phrases you have learned in this unit. *Practice > Unit 2 > Activity 17*

Check (✓) the skills you learned. If you need more work on a skill, refer to the page(s) in parentheses.

NOTE-TAKING ☐ I can use visual elements. (p. 26)

LISTENING ☐ I can understand cause and effect. (p. 31)

CRITICAL THINKING ☐ I can evaluate cause-and-effect statements. (p. 32)

VOCABULARY ☐ I can use noun and verb word families. (p. 39)

GRAMMAR ☐ I can use *there's* and *it's*. (p. 41)

PRONUNCIATION ☐ I can use the schwa in unstressed syllables. (p. 42)

SPEAKING ☐ I can ask for and give examples. (p. 43)

OBJECTIVE ▶ ☐ I can gather information and ideas to participate in a group presentation about the uses of color.

3 Social Psychology

LISTENING	predicting
CRITICAL THINKING	applying what you learn
NOTE-TAKING	organizing notes
VOCABULARY	synonyms
GRAMMAR	modal verbs *should* and *shouldn't*
PRONUNCIATION	final /s/ or /z/ sounds
SPEAKING	giving advice and making recommendations

Why are social skills important?

A. Discuss these questions with your classmates.

1. What are social skills? Give examples.

2. Are you ever unsure about what to do in social situations? Give examples.

3. Look at the photo. What are some things we do to make social situations easier?

B. Listen to *The Q Classroom* online. Then answer these questions.

1. What does Yuna say about social skills?

2. What ideas do Sophy and Felix add to Yuna's?

3. What kind of course did Marcus take?

iQ PRACTICE Go to the online discussion board to discuss the Unit Question with your classmates. *Practice > Unit 3 > Activity 1*

UNIT OBJECTIVE

Listen to a radio program and a news report. Gather information and ideas to give a presentation about manners.

LISTENING 1

OBJECTIVE ▶

Be Polite

You are going to listen to a radio program called *Book Talk*. The people on the program talk about the book *The Civility Solution: What to Do When People Are Rude* by P. M. Forni. It is about the need for more polite behavior in our society. As you listen, gather information and ideas about why social skills are important.

PREVIEW THE LISTENING

A. VOCABULARY Here are some words from Listening 1. Read the definitions. Then circle the best word to complete each sentence.

behavior *(noun)* 🔑 OPAL the way you act

courtesy *(noun)* pleasant behavior that shows respect for other people

etiquette *(noun)* the rules for courtesy and polite behavior

manners *(noun)* 🔑 acceptable behavior in a culture

polite *(adjective)* 🔑 having good manners and showing courtesy

rude *(adjective)* 🔑 not polite

🔑 Oxford 3000™ words   OPAL Oxford Phrasal Academic Lexicon

1. You should always treat coworkers with (behavior /(courtesy)) and respect. Good manners are important at work.

2. Miteb's (behavior / courtesy) in today's class was terrible. He arrived late, he talked on his cell phone, and then he went to sleep!

3. I'm nervous about dining in the restaurant tonight. There are so many different glasses and forks on the table. Can I borrow your book about (etiquette / behavior)?

4. When you stay at a friend's house, it is (polite / rude) to write him or her a thank-you note. It shows you are a good friend.

5. That child was very rude to everyone. Parents should teach their kids better (manners / courtesy).

VOCABULARY SKILL REVIEW

In Unit 2, you learned that some words can be used as a noun or a verb. Circle the underlined words in Activity B that can be used as both a noun and a verb.

B. IDENTIFY Read the sentences. Then choose the answer that best matches the meaning of each underlined word.

1. I admit that I made a mistake. I was rude to Sara.

   a. agree it is true

   b. think it is wrong

2. Different cultures and groups of people have different ideas about what's OK. In that society, it's normal for people to arrive late.

   a. a group of people at a school

   b. the people of one country or area

3. There have been more accidents lately. One reason for the increase in car accidents is that people don't pay attention to the road.

   a. smaller number

   b. growing number

4. There's too much violence in video games. It's not good to see characters fight and kill.

   a. rude or impolite words

   b. actions done to hurt someone

5. When a soccer player scores a goal, the people in the stadium often scream with excitement. The noise is incredible!

   a. speak in very loud voices

   b. speak very quietly

iQ PRACTICE Go online for more practice with the vocabulary.
Practice > Unit 3 > Activities 2–3

As a listener, you can't always **predict**, or guess, what you are going to hear. There's no way to know what people are going to talk about at an event or what you are going to hear on the street. At other times, you can predict the topic—for example, in a class, on TV, or on the radio. In these cases, you can prepare to listen.

- Find out about the topic. For a radio or TV program, look at the program guide. For a class, check the class schedule or your notes from the last class.

- Ask, "What do I know about this topic?"

For example, if you are going to watch a TV documentary about tigers, you might ask questions like these.

What do I know about tigers?

What do they look like?

Where do they live?

Road rage

C. PREVIEW You are going to listen to people on a radio program talk about the need for more polite behavior in our society. What do you think is the best way to respond to a rude person? Discuss your idea with a partner.

D. DISCUSS Listen to three parts of the radio program. Before you listen to each part, discuss the question with a partner. Predict what the speaker will say. Listen to check your prediction.

Part 1 The host of the program is going to introduce his guest. What information do you think he will include?

Part 2 What question did the host ask at the end of Part 1? How do you think Lynn Hancock will answer this question?

Part 3 How does the host feel about being polite when others are rude? What will Hancock say about this?

iQ PRACTICE Go online for more practice with predicting.
Practice › Unit 3 › Activity 4

iQ PRACTICE Go online for additional listening and comprehension.
Practice › Unit 3 › Activity 5

WORK WITH THE LISTENING

A. LISTEN AND TAKE NOTES Listen to the program again. As you listen, think about these key words and phrases. Why is each one important? Use the words in your notes.

bad manners	polite	the "civility solution"	road rage
increase	rudeness	journalist	violence

B. CATEGORIZE Read the statements. Write *T* (true) or *F* (false). Use your notes to help you.

_____ 1. Professor Forni says people are more polite now than in the past.

_____ 2. Professor Forni says rudeness can cause social problems.

_____ 3. Professor Forni says there is no connection between rudeness and stress.

_____ 4. The best idea is to be polite when people are rude to you.

_____ 5. It's OK to say that you don't like someone's behavior.

TIP FOR SUCCESS

As you listen, try to think ahead. Ask, "What's next? What is the speaker going to say?"

C. IDENTIFY Read the sentences. Choose the answer that best completes each statement. Then listen and check your answers.

1. The host of the program is _____.

   a. Scott Webber

   b. John Hopkins

   c. Lynn Hancock

2. "Road rage" is a term used to describe drivers who _____.

   a. get angry while driving

   b. are not good drivers

   c. drive too fast

3. If someone is yelling at you, you should _____.

   a. scream at them

   b. say nothing and walk away

   c. stay calm and speak politely

4. Lynn tells a story about something that happened to her when she was _____.

   a. driving her car

   b. riding on a bus

   c. riding on the subway

D. EXPLAIN Lynn Hancock tells a story to show how the "civility solution" worked for her. Work with a partner. Take turns asking and answering the questions.

1. What happened?

2. Was it an accident or did she do it on purpose?

3. What did the man do?

4. How did Lynn respond?

5. Was the "civility solution" successful in this case?

 E. IDENTIFY Work in a group. Read the excerpt from Listening 1 and fill in the missing words. Then listen and check your answers.

Well, that's where the "civility _____(1)_____" comes in. When someone

is _____(2)_____ to us, it's natural, or _____(3)_____,

to be rude to them. You're rude to me, so I'm rude to you. It's a

_____(4)_____ of rudeness. But, when we're _____(5)_____

to someone who is rude, it _____(6)_____ the circle. In other

_____(7)_____, you're rude to me, but I'm polite to you. If people can

learn to do this, our _____(8)_____ will be better.

CRITICAL THINKING STRATEGY

Applying what you learn

Sometimes understanding what you hear—for example, in a lecture or a conversation—is not enough. You may need to apply what you learn to real-life situations. For example, in a math class, you learn skills you may need for your job or solving problems around your home. In a history class, you learn about events from the past. Then you can compare these with events today and think about what we can learn from the past.

In the following activities, you will explore how you might apply Professor Forni's ideas and your learning to new situations.

iQ PRACTICE Go online to watch the Critical Thinking Video and check your comprehension. *Practice > Unit 3 > Activity 6*

F. **CREATE** Work with a partner. Choose one of these situations. Create a conversation to practice the civility solution. One person will be A and the other will be B. Use these examples to get you started.

Situation 1: A meeting of coworkers in an office to discuss ways to make the office a better place to work.

A: Suggest that workers collect money to buy a coffee machine for the office.

A: *We really need a new coffee machine for the office. If we all give five dollars, we can buy one.*

B: Say that A's idea is "ridiculous."

A: Respond to B. Use the civility solution.

Situation 2: Two people sitting next to each other on a train. There's a sign above the seats that says "As a courtesy to other passengers, please do not use your cell phone on the train."

A: You are talking loudly to a friend on your cell phone.

A: *Hi, you know we had a great time yesterday at . . .*

B: Ask A politely to stop talking on the cell phone. Point to the sign.

A: Tell B that you will stop "in a minute," but keep on talking.

B: Ask A to stop talking on the cell phone. Be polite, but firm. Use the civility solution.

G. **DISCUSS** Act out your conversation for the class. How are your classmates' conversations similar to or different from yours? Discuss as a class.

 SAY WHAT YOU THINK

DISCUSS Discuss the questions in a small group.

1. Think of a time when someone was rude to you. What did you do and say?

2. What do you think of Professor Forni's ideas? Are they easy to follow? Do they work? Why or why not?

3. Imagine that many people start to follow Professor Forni's ideas. Can this change society?

NOTE-TAKING SKILL Organizing notes

When you take notes, it is important to organize the notes on the page. First, write the topic at the top of the page. Do this before the class begins if you can. When the class begins, make a quick outline for your notes. For example, an instructor might say something like, "Today we're going to talk about three ways in which rudeness hurts individuals and our society." This tells you that there are three main points to listen for. If this happens, write the numbers 1, 2, 3 on the page. Leave space after each number to write notes.

Read the introduction to a presentation about the use of color in architecture. Notice that the student wrote a few key words about the topic at the top of the page. The student then prepared space for the two main topics in the discussion and copied the names the instructor wrote on the board.

> Today we're going to discuss the work of two architects and their use of color. First, you will see some examples of the work of the Mexican architect Luis Barragán. Then we'll move on to the work of young French architect Emmanuelle Moureaux. Moureaux's use of happy colors in her work makes some refer to her as a "Joymaker."

architecture, use of color

1. Luis Barragán

2. Emmanuelle Moureaux

 A. APPLY Listen to the introduction to a talk titled "A History of Rude Behavior." Then prepare a page you could use to take notes.

B. EXTEND Compare your note page with a partner. Answer the questions.

1. How many topics did the speaker mention?

2. How did you describe each topic?

iQ PRACTICE Go online for more practice with organizing notes.
Practice ⟩ Unit 3 ⟩ Activity 7

LISTENING 2   Classroom Etiquette

OBJECTIVE ▶   You are going to listen to a news report about teaching etiquette in the classroom. Teachers think that students need to learn better manners. The question is, "Who should teach manners, parents or teachers?" As you listen, gather information and ideas about why social skills are important.

PREVIEW THE LISTENING

A. VOCABULARY   Here are some words and phrases from Listening 2. Read the definitions. Then complete each sentence with the correct word or phrase.

attentive *(adjective)* watching or listening carefully

courteous *(adjective)* polite, having courtesy

deal with *(verb phrase)* to solve a problem

improve *(verb)* 🔑 OPAL to make something better

influence *(noun)* 🔑 OPAL the power to change how someone or something acts

principal *(noun)* the person in charge of a school

respect *(noun)* 🔑 OPAL consideration for the rights and feelings of other people

shout out *(verb phrase)* to say something in a loud voice

valuable *(adjective)* 🔑 OPAL very useful or important

🔑 Oxford 3000™ words   **OPAL** Oxford Phrasal Academic Lexicon

1. I apologized to show Sue I have _____ for her feelings.

2. The parents are meeting with the _____ tonight to discuss problems at school. She can make new school rules to stop the problems.

3. Parents can have a great _____ on a child's behavior. They can teach by setting an example.

4. Teachers have to _____ many difficult problems in the classroom every day. They think of many good solutions.

5. Everyone thought that the class was very _____. It helped them get better grades and it improved their social skills.

6. I don't like it when people in a meeting just _____ their comments. They should wait their turn and speak politely.

7. Lisa and Mark want to _____ their Spanish. They go to class every day and practice often.

8. Young children can only be _____ for 20 or 30 minutes at a time. It is hard for them to sit still and focus for a long time.

9. Your son is very _____ at school. He calls me Ms. Moore, and he always says *please* and *thank you*.

iQ PRACTICE Go online for more practice with the vocabulary.
Practice > Unit 3 > Activities 8–9

B. PREVIEW You are going to listen to a news report about teaching etiquette in the classroom. What do you think parents and teachers say about the etiquette classes? Choose *a* or *b*. Then explain your choice to a partner.

a. They like the classes. They feel they have a positive effect on the children's behavior.

b. The classes are a waste of time. Kids have to learn good manners at home.

WORK WITH THE LISTENING

A. LISTEN AND TAKE NOTES Prepare a page for note-taking. Write a few key words and a short outline. Then listen to the first part of the news report about teaching etiquette in the classroom.

B. APPLY Listen to the rest of the news report and take notes. Use the page you prepared in Activity A.

C. APPLY Read the sentences. Choose the answer that best completes each statement. Use your notes to help you.

1. The main point of the news report is that ____.

   a. parents don't know how to teach their children good manners

   b. teachers don't have time to teach manners in the classroom

   c. some schools teach manners in the classroom

2. According to Marjorie Lucas, the most important idea about manners is that ____.

   a. children need to respect other people

   b. fighting and violence are bad

   c. children need to have good table manners

3. The report makes it clear that ____.

   a. parents are better than schools at teaching manners

   b. the results of the etiquette classes surprised teachers

   c. the etiquette classes helped children, teachers, and parents

D. IDENTIFY Work with a partner. Try to find information in your notes about each of these items. Listen again and add to your notes, if necessary.

1. one example of polite behavior for children around adults

2. the name of the company that teaches etiquette classes

3. one example of good behavior at school

4. two positive results from the etiquette classes

5. how parents feel about the etiquette classes

E. EVALUATE Listen to four sentences from the news report. Choose the sentence that is closest in meaning to the one you hear.

1. a. When teachers have to spend time dealing with bad behavior, they have less time to teach other things.

   b. For teachers, dealing with bad behavior is the most important part of their job.

2. a. When children do small things, like saying "please" and "thank you," it shows that they have respect for others.

   b. Children can be courteous in small ways, but that doesn't mean they respect other people.

3. a. Students earned good grades in the etiquette classes during the school year.

   b. Because of the etiquette classes, students got better grades in their classwork.

4. a. Students listen more carefully when they are in class.

   b. Students aren't absent from class as much as they were in the past.

F. CREATE Look at the list of rules that a teacher made for the classroom. Complete each sentence on the list with a phrase from the box. Then add one more "rule" to the list. Use your own idea.

get into fights	shout out the answer	say "Excuse me"
raise your hand	Mr., Ms., or Mrs.	say "Thank you"
say "Please"		

CLASSROOM RULES

1. When you want to answer a question, _raise your hand_ .

2. Don't _____ when I ask a question.

3. When you speak to teachers or to the principal, use _____ and their last name.

4. If you bump into someone, _____.

5. When you ask for something, _____.

6. Don't _____ in the hallway or on the playground.

7. When someone gives you something, _____.

8. _____

WORK WITH THE VIDEO

A. PREVIEW Before you watch the video on making "small talk," discuss this question with a partner: How do you feel when you are in room with a lot of people you don't know?

VIDEO VOCABULARY

rapport (n.) a friendly situation in which people understand each other

initiate (v.) to start something

snippet (n.) a small piece of something

confidence (n.) trust or belief in someone or something

contentious debate (n.) angry argument

iQ RESOURCES Go online to watch the video about a class learning the social skill of making "small talk." *Resources > Video > Unit 3 > Unit Video*

B. CATEGORIZE Watch the video two or three times and take notes. Then read the statements. Write *T* (true) or *F* (false). Use your notes to help you.

____ 1. The expert says that "small talk" has that name because it isn't important.

____ 2. Small talk helps build rapport among people.

____ 3. A tag line is a type of question.

____ 4. A passive participant in a conversation asks questions.

____ 5. Small talk should include comments about your health problems.

____ 6. It's not OK to get into a big argument with someone you just met.

____ 7. People who are good at small talk enjoy conversations more.

____ 8. People who are good at small talk make better connections.

C. EXTEND Do you agree that the ability to make small talk is an important social skill? Why or why not? Discuss the questions in a small group. Give examples to support your opinion.

SAY WHAT YOU THINK

SYNTHESIZE Think about the unit video, Listening 1, and Listening 2 as you discuss the questions.

1. How did you learn about etiquette and social skills? Did you learn from your parents? Teachers? Other sources? Give examples.

2. What would Professor Forni think about companies giving etiquette classes in schools?

3. Marjorie Lucas, from the company Polite Children, said, "In the end, manners are all about having respect for others." How can you apply this idea in your daily life?

Words with the same or very similar meanings are called **synonyms**. Synonyms can make your speaking and writing more interesting.

Dictionaries show the meanings of synonyms, and they provide helpful examples about how to use synonyms.

Dictionaries often give synonyms at the end of entries, and the example sentences at different entries show you how to use the words correctly. For example, look at these definitions of the words *anger* and *rage*. *Anger* and *rage* are synonyms, but *rage* is a stronger feeling than *anger*.

anger¹ /ˈæŋɡər/ *noun* [U] the strong feeling that you have when something has happened or someone has done something that you do not like: *He could not hide his anger at the news.* ♦ *She was shaking with anger.*

rage¹ /reɪdʒ/ *noun* [C, U] a feeling of violent anger that is difficult to control: *He was trembling with rage.* ♦ *to fly into a rage*

All dictionary entries adapted from the *Oxford American Dictionary for learners of English* © Oxford University Press 2011.

A. APPLY Match each word on the left with a synonym on the right. Use your dictionary to help you.

_____ 1. courteous   a. growth

_____ 2. rude   b. impolite

_____ 3. scream   c. polite

_____ 4. valuable   d. yell

_____ 5. etiquette   e. manners

_____ 6. increase   f. important

B. RESTATE Synonyms work well in these sentences. Rewrite each sentence using a synonym for the word or words in bold.

1. I think it's **rude** to use your cell phone on the bus.

   I think it's impolite to use your cell phone on the bus.

2. Please tell the kids outside to stop **screaming**. My students are taking a test.

   _____

3. If salespeople are **courteous**, they'll probably make more sales.

   _____

4. Emily Post wrote many books about **good manners**.

   _____

iQ PRACTICE Go online for more practice with synonyms.
Practice > Unit 3 > Activity 10

SPEAKING

OBJECTIVE ▶

At the end of this unit, you are going to work in a group to give a presentation about using manners in a particular situation. As part of the presentation, you will have to give advice about what people should and should not do in the situation.

GRAMMAR Modal verbs *should* and *shouldn't*

Use **should** and **shouldn't** to give and ask for *advice* and *recommendations*.

Affirmative: You **should** be polite, even when someone is rude to you.
☐ You **should** wear a suit and tie to the interview.

Negative: We **shouldn't** let people say rude things to us.
☐ You **shouldn't** speak Spanish when Ron is here. He doesn't understand it.

Questions: **Should** our listeners read the book?
☐ What **should** we do about the kids who wrote on the wall at school?

iQ RESOURCES Go online to watch the Grammar Skill Video.
Resources > Video > Unit 3 > Grammar Skill Video

A. APPLY Complete each sentence with *should* or *shouldn't*. Use your own opinions.

1. Your best friend thinks she is sending an email to her parents. She sends it to you by mistake. You _____ read it.

2. A woman _____ open the door for a man carrying a large box.

3. Children _____ call their teachers by their first names.

4. University students _____ raise their hands to ask a question in class.

5. You _____ call people after 10 p.m.

6. Men _____ stand up when a woman comes into the room.

7. You _____ tell someone if they have spinach in their teeth.

8. You're sitting on a crowded bus. An older woman gets on. You _____ offer her your seat.

B. EXPLAIN Work with a partner. Take turns asking and answering *Yes/No* questions based on the sentences in Activity A. Explain your answers.

A: *Should you read your friend's email to her parents?*
B: *No, you shouldn't. You should tell your friend about it.*

SPEAKING **61**

iQ PRACTICE Go online for more practice with the modal verbs *should* and *shouldn't*. *Practice > Unit 3 > Activity 11*

iQ PRACTICE Go online for the Grammar Expansion: modal verbs *have to* and *has to*. *Practice > Unit 3 > Activity 12*

PRONUNCIATION Final /s/ or /z/ sounds

Words ending in /s/ or /z/ sounds link, or connect, to words beginning with a vowel. Listen to these examples.

It's easy to make small talk.

The man was mad at the other drivers around him.

A. IDENTIFY Read the sentences. Mark the /s/ and /z/ sounds that link to vowels.

1. The students admitted they made a mistake.

2. Parents are too busy to teach their children manners.

3. The book talks about different ways to deal with problems.

4. Bad manners are a problem in our office.

5. I was amazed by my visit to the Great Wall.

6. Is it possible for them to deal with the problem today?

TIP FOR SUCCESS

Learning how to link words will make your speech sound more natural and fluent. It can also make it easier to pronounce final sounds clearly.

B. APPLY Work with a partner. Practice saying the sentences in Activity A. Listen and check your pronunciation.

C. EXTEND Listen to the paragraph about the etiquette of hats. Complete the paragraph with the words you hear. Then read the story to a partner.

Franklin D. Roosevelt, 1944

John F. Kennedy, 1963

THE ETIQUETTE OF HATS

There are a lot of _____ about _____ in etiquette books.
                        1   2

_____ _____, men and women always wore _____
          3   4   5

_____. It was bad _____ to go out without a hat. Men took off their
          6   7

_____ _____. It _____ _____ sign of
          8   9   10   11

respect for a man to take off his hat. These rules started to change in the 1960s. John F. Kennedy was

the first U.S. president to appear in public without a hat.

iQ PRACTICE   Go online for more practice with final /s/ or /z/ sounds.
Practice ▶ Unit 3 ▶ Activity 13

SPEAKING SKILL   Giving advice and making recommendations

When you give **advice** or make **recommendations**, you don't want the listener
to think that you're giving commands. To make sure the listener understands,
you can use expressions like these.

> I think you should . . .
> I don't think you should . . .
> Don't you think you should . . . ?
> Maybe you shouldn't . . .

A. CREATE Work with a partner. Read the sentences. Take turns giving advice.

1. **A:** It is hard to get to class on time. What should I do?

   B: I think you should . . .

2. **A:** My homework is very messy. It is difficult for the teacher to read.

   B: Don't you think you should . . . ?

3. **A:** Alan invited me to his house for dinner, but I don't know anybody there!

   B: Maybe you should/shouldn't . . .

4. **A:** My friends send me text messages when I'm in class. It's hard to pay
   attention in class when they send me messages.

   B: Well, I don't think you should . . .

B. EXTEND Work with a partner. Choose one of the topics below. Ask your partner for advice. Then give your partner advice about the problem he or she chooses.

1. You are going to a formal dinner at someone's home. Ask for advice about what to wear, what time to arrive, what to bring, what to talk about with guests, and table manners.

2. You are in charge of a committee. The committee's job is to improve your workplace or classroom. The goal is to encourage people to be more courteous to each other. Ask for advice about what the committee should do.

iQ PRACTICE Go online for more practice with giving advice and making recommendations. *Practice > Unit 3 > Activity 14*

UNIT ASSIGNMENT Give a presentation on manners

OBJECTIVE ▶

In this section, you are going to give a short presentation about manners. As you prepare your presentation, think about the Unit Question, "Why are social skills important?" Use information from Listening 1, Listening 2, the unit video, and your work in this unit to support your presentation. Refer to the Self-Assessment checklist on page 66.

CONSIDER THE IDEAS

EVALUATE Read the list of statements and check (✓) the ones you agree with.

☐ People don't always need to have good manners.

☐ I think people should learn proper etiquette.

☐ Manners should be taught at home, not at school.

☐ I prefer to be with people who have good manners.

☐ People should know how to behave at all times.

☐ Good table manners are not very important.

PREPARE AND SPEAK

A. GATHER IDEAS Work in a group. Choose one presentation topic from the box or think of your own topic.

Bad manners for . . .
• children at home
• driving a car
• eating with family or friends
• riding on a train or bus
• students in the classroom

B. ORGANIZE IDEAS Prepare a short presentation on the topic your group picked in Activity A. Use the outline to help you organize your ideas. Give at least two examples.

Topic: Bad manners for _____

1. What some people do: _____

    Why is this an example of bad manners?

    Reasons:

    a. _____

    b. _____

    What people should do: _____

    Reasons:

    a. _____

    b. _____

2. What some people do: _____

    Why is this an example of bad manners?

    Reasons:

    a. _____

    b. _____

    What people should do: _____

    Reasons:

    a. _____

    b. _____

C. **SPEAK** Present your ideas to the class or to another group. Refer to the Self-Assessment checklist below before you begin.

1. Make sure each member of your group presents at least one idea in the presentation. For example, one person can describe an example of bad manners.

2. In your presentation, explain:
   - why you chose the topic.
   - examples of bad manners.
   - why the behaviors are bad.
   - how people should behave.

iQ PRACTICE Go online for your alternate Unit Assignment.
Practice > Unit 3 > Activity 15

CHECK AND REFLECT

A. CHECK Think about the Unit Assignment as you complete the Self-Assessment checklist.

SELF-ASSESSMENT	Yes	No
I was able to speak easily about the topic.	☐	☐
My group or class understood me.	☐	☐
I used *should* and *shouldn't*.	☐	☐
I used vocabulary from the unit.	☐	☐
I gave advice and I made recommendations.	☐	☐
I connected final /s/ and /z/ sounds to vowels.	☐	☐

B. REFLECT Discuss these questions with a partner or group.

1. What is something new you learned in this unit?

2. Look back at the Unit Question—Why are social skills important? Is your answer different now than when you started this unit? If yes, how is it different? Why?

iQ PRACTICE Go to the online discussion board to discuss these questions.
Practice > Unit 3 > Activity 16

TRACK YOUR SUCCESS

iQ PRACTICE Go online to check the words and phrases you have learned in this unit. *Practice > Unit 3 > Activity 17*

Check (✓) the skills you learned. If you need more work on a skill, refer to the page(s) in parentheses.

LISTENING	☐ I can predict. (p. 50)
CRITICAL THINKING	☐ I can apply what I've learned. (p. 52)
NOTE-TAKING	☐ I can organize notes. (p. 54)
VOCABULARY	☐ I can use synonyms. (p. 60)
GRAMMAR	☐ I can use the modal verbs *should* and *shouldn't*. (p. 61)
PRONUNCIATION	☐ I can connect final /s/ or /z/ sounds. (p. 62)
SPEAKING	☐ I can give advice and make recommendations. (p. 63)

OBJECTIVE ▶   ☐ I can gather information and ideas to give a presentation about social skills.

Technology

4

NOTE-TAKING	using symbols and abbreviations
CRITICAL THINKING	curiosity
LISTENING	listening for specific information
VOCABULARY	using the dictionary
GRAMMAR	comparatives
PRONUNCIATION	linking between consonant sounds
SPEAKING	asking for and giving clarification

How does technology affect our relationships?

A. Discuss these questions with your classmates.

1. What kinds of electronic devices do you use every day? Examples include cell phones and GPS trackers.

2. About how many hours each day do you spend using these devices at work? At school? At home?

3. Look at the picture. When you're with your friends or family, do you spend more time talking or using an electronic device?

B. Listen to *The Q Classroom* online. Then match the ideas to the students.

_____ 1. We still need face time with each other.   a. Felix

_____ 2. It's easier to keep in touch with friends.   b. Sophy

_____ 3. My friends and I don't talk like we used to.   c. Marcus

_____ 4. We have one night a week as family night.   d. Yuna

iQ PRACTICE   Go to the online discussion board to discuss the Unit Question with your classmates. *Practice > Unit 4 > Activity 1*

UNIT OBJECTIVE

Listen to a lecture and a conversation. Gather information and ideas to participate in a panel discussion about how technology affects our relationships.

NOTE-TAKING SKILL Using symbols and abbreviations

Many people now communicate by texting each other on their cell phones. To save time when they text, people use symbols and shortened forms of common words and expressions. Symbols and abbreviations are also useful for note-taking. The following list has some common symbols and abbreviations.

=	*equals, is the same as*	**w, w/o**	*with, without*
&	*and*	**etc.**	*and so on, and more*
e.g.	*for example*	**+**	*plus, more than*
re	*about*	**v.**	*very*

You can also create your own abbreviations. Abbreviate long words or frequently repeated words. Use initials for the names of people or organizations after the first use. Write numbers as numerals instead of words, e.g., 4 (not *four*). Just be sure that you can remember what your abbreviations stand for!

A. COMPOSE Read this student's notes about an inventor. Write a complete version of what you think the notes say. Then compare with a partner.

> Alex. Graham Bell b. 1847 Scot. scientist
>
> 1870 moved to Canada, prov. of Ontario & set up workshop
>
> 1874 Ass't was Thomas Watson
>
> 1876 invent. 1st working tel. w/ TW's help
>
> Mar. 10 '76 1st tel. call. AGB called TW (in next room)
>   said "Mr. W. come here, I want you."
>
> 1877 AGB start Bell Tel. Co.
>
> 1886 150,000+ in US have tel. in home

B. APPLY Listen to this short talk about the telegraph invented by Samuel Morse. Take notes using symbols and abbreviations.

iQ PRACTICE Go online for more practice with using symbols and abbreviations to take notes. *Practice ⟩ Unit 4 ⟩ Activity 2*

LISTENING 1

OBJECTIVE ▶

Online Friendships

You are going to listen to a lecture about social media and friendship. As you listen, gather information and ideas about how technology affects our relationships.

PREVIEW THE LISTENING

A. VOCABULARY Here are some words and phrases from Listening 1. Read the definitions. Then complete each sentence with the correct word or phrase.

TIP FOR SUCCESS
Focus on listening for these words and phrases when you listen for the first time.

face-to-face *(adjective phrase / adverb phrase)* close to and looking at someone or something

forever *(adverb)* 🔑 for all time; permanently

friendship *(noun)* 🔑 the state of being friends

headline *(noun)* 🔑 the title of a newspaper or magazine article printed in large letters above the story

meaningful *(adjective)* OPAL useful, important, or interesting

post *(verb)* 🔑 to put information or pictures on a website

privacy 🔑 *(noun)* the state of being free from the attention of the public

relationship *(noun)* 🔑 OPAL a connection between two people or things

🔑 Oxford 3000™ words   **OPAL** Oxford Phrasal Academic Lexicon

1. You don't have to be best friends, but it is important to have a good

   _____ with your coworkers.

2. Dora finished writing the article last night. It's ready to _____

   online.

3. We need curtains on those windows. Without them, we have no

   _____ in the bedroom.

4. It is hard to discuss some things online. You need a _____

   conversation where you can see the other person.

ACADEMIC LANGUAGE

The word *relationship* is often used in academic contexts. Notice that the suffix *-ship* is also used in the noun *friendship*. The suffix *-ship* indicates a state or condition.

_____ OPAL

Oxford Phrasal Academic Lexicon

5. His _____ with Tom is very important to Reza. They have

   known each other for many years.

6. The newspaper _____ said that there will be bad snowstorms

   in the Midwest today.

7. Their family has lived here _____. I mean a very long time,

   more than 100 years.

8. The lecturer made some very _____ statements about social

   media. It gave me a lot to think about.

iQ PRACTICE   Go online for more practice with the vocabulary.
Practice > Unit 4 > Activities 3–4

B. PREVIEW You are going to listen to a lecture about social media and friendship. Work with a partner. List one good thing and one possible problem related to social media and friendships.

WORK WITH THE LISTENING

A. LISTEN AND TAKE NOTES Listen to Part 1 of the lecture. The speaker mentions three points that will be in the lecture. Prepare a piece of paper to take notes. List the three points and leave space for writing after each one.

iQ RESOURCES Go online to download extra vocabulary support.
Resources › Extra Vocabulary › Unit 4

B. LISTEN AND TAKE NOTES Listen to Part 2 of the lecture. Take notes. Use symbols and abbreviations to save time.

C. INTERPRET Check (✓) the three sentences that best express the main ideas of the lecture. Use your notes to help you.

- ☐ 1. Most people will continue to use social media to communicate with friends.
- ☐ 2. Robin Dunbar usually prefers talking to friends face-to-face, not online.
- ☐ 3. Some users of social media visit the sites several times each day.
- ☐ 4. The use of social media is changing the way people think about friendship.
- ☐ 5. Sixty-nine percent of adults in the United States have online friends.
- ☐ 6. One danger of social media is that users can lose control of private information.

D. APPLY Listen to Part 2 again. Write the correct number to complete each sentence.

1. In 2018, _____ percent of people in the United States between the ages of 18 and 29 used social media.

2. Worldwide, about _____ _____ people used social media.

3. The speaker says that no one can have meaningful relationships with _____ people.

4. Robin Dunbar did a study of more than _____ people.

5. Most people in this group had about _____ online friends.

6. Of this number of online friends, usually fewer than _____ were close friends.

E. EVALUATE Think about the speaker in Listening 1. Would this person agree or disagree with the following statements? Do you agree or disagree with them? Complete the chart using *A* (agree) or *D* (disagree).

Statement	Speaker	You
1. Online friends aren't real friends.		
2. People should never post personal information online.		
3. Social media can be fun and useful if used carefully.		

F. EXPLAIN Compare answers with a partner. Are your answers the same or different? Explain and discuss.

 CRITICAL THINKING STRATEGY

Curiosity

Curiosity is a desire to know or to learn something. Critical thinking requires a curious mind. This means that curious learners do not accept everything they hear as true just because the speaker said it. They also want to know more about the speaker's topic. They ask questions that might start like this:

What did you mean when you said . . . ?

Why did you say that . . . ?

Do you have more information about . . . ?

Where did the statistic about ____ come from?

iQ PRACTICE Go online to watch the Critical Thinking Video and check your comprehension. *Practice > Unit 4 > Activity 5*

 G. CREATE Listen again to part of Listening 1. Write two questions you would like to ask the speaker.

1. _____

2. _____

H. EXTEND Work with a partner. Share the questions you created in Activity G. How do you think the speaker might answer them? Discuss.

iQ PRACTICE Go online for additional listening and comprehension. *Practice > Unit 4 > Activity 6*

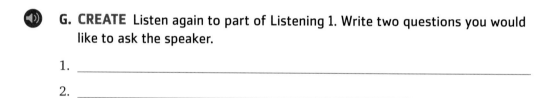 # SAY WHAT YOU THINK

DISCUSS Discuss the questions in a small group.

1. Were you surprised about the number of people who use social media? Why or why not?

2. How do you think that social media might affect friendships?

3. What are some problems you or your friends experience with social media sites?

LISTENING SKILL Listening for specific information

Sometimes you need to listen for a specific piece of information. To listen for **specific information**, focus on key words. The answer to a question is often just before or after a key word from the question.

You need to know: How many social media users were there worldwide in 2018?

The key word: worldwide

☐ **You hear: Worldwide**, about **2.62 billion** people used social media in 2018.

The answer: 2.62 billion

 A. IDENTIFY Read the questions. Then listen to the statements from Listening 1. Focus on the key words. Answer the questions.

1. What is the **average number** of friends each person had in Dunbar's study?

_____

TIP FOR SUCCESS
Practice listening in English as often as possible. At times, you may only understand a few words, but even this can improve your skills.

2. What was **the point of** the newspaper article with the **headline**, "Nobody has real friends anymore."

_____

3. How did some users compare **online discussions** with ones they had **face-to-face**?

_____

 B. IDENTIFY Read the questions and focus on the words in bold. Listen to a short talk about a photographer named Tanja Hollander. Listen for the bold words to find the information.

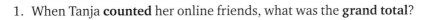

1. When Tanja **counted** her online friends, what was the **grand total**?

_____

2. Where **were these friends from**?

_____

Tanja Hollander

3. What did Tanja **decide** to do?

_____

4. How many **years** did it take her to complete her project?

_____

5. **Where** did she go to visit an old college friend, the **poet and hip-hop artist**?

_____

iQ PRACTICE Go online for more practice listening for specific information.
Practice > Unit 4 > Activity 7

Who Are You Talking To?

You are going to listen to a conversation about electronic devices that "talk" to us. As you listen, gather information and ideas about how technology affects our relationships.

PREVIEW THE LISTENING

VOCABULARY SKILL REVIEW

In Unit 3, you learned about synonyms. Some of the correct answers in Activity A are one-word synonyms for the underlined words. Can you identify at least three of these synonyms?

A. VOCABULARY Here are some words and phrases from Listening 2. Read the sentences. Then choose the answer that best matches the meaning of each <u>underlined</u> word or phrase.

1. Since the camera on my smartphone is so good, I rarely use a separate <u>digital</u> camera these days.

   a. easy to carry   b. using computer technology

2. I'm not going to wear that <u>silly</u> hat! Everyone will laugh.

   a. ugly   b. crazy

3. When we got home, we <u>found</u> that the front door was open and our TV was gone!

   a. discovered   b. thought

4. Ronnie sometimes has rather <u>strange</u> ideas about how to do things.

   a. unusual   b. bad

5. I closed my eyes during that part of the movie. It was too <u>scary</u>.

   a. boring   b. frightening

6. The American robin is a <u>common</u> bird. You see them frequently in the spring, summer, and fall.

   a. pretty   b. usual

7. We've become very <u>dependent on</u> our computers in the workplace. We can't function without them.

   a. needing something   b. unhappy about

8. I've <u>disconnected</u> the cable TV in our house. We were watching it too much.

   a. repaired a problem with   b. stopped the service for

iQ PRACTICE   Go online for more practice with the vocabulary.
Practice > Unit 4 > Activities 8–9

B. **PREVIEW** In the twenty-first century, more and more people use digital devices in their daily lives. Some digital assistants can even "talk" to us. You are going to listen to a conversation that includes a discussion of GPS trackers in cars. Have you used a GPS for driving directions? Discuss with a partner.

WORK WITH THE LISTENING

TIP FOR SUCCESS

When listening, take very short notes to help you remember what you hear. Write only single words or short phrases. Then complete your notes later.

A. **CREATE** The words and phrases below are key words in the conversation. Think of an abbreviation you can use for each one when you take notes.

1. artificial voices   _____

2. artificial intelligence _____

3. voice-activated device   _____

4. smart devices   _____

5. too dependent on   _____

6. invention   _____

B. **LISTEN AND TAKE NOTES** Listen to the conversation and take notes. Use the abbreviations you listed in Activity A.

C. **IDENTIFY** Choose the description that best summarizes all the main ideas of the conversation.

_____ 1. Digital devices that speak to us are taking the place of the people in our lives by doing things for us and talking with us.

_____ 2. Digital devices can be helpful, but we should remember that they are not human.

_____ 3. Digital devices improve our lives by doing things like giving us directions, doing tasks around the house, and helping people feel less lonely.

D. EXPLAIN Answer the questions. Use your notes to help you. Then listen again and check your answers.

1. Why is Leo frustrated with the GPS voice?

   _____

2. What does Aran say about artificial voices?

   _____

3. What does Aran's daughter ask the device she calls "Susie" in their home?

   _____

4. What is one task in the home that a voice-activated device can do?

   _____

5. What did Leo's friends do when they found the device talking to itself?

   _____

6. What other invention does Leo mention that changed how people live?

   _____

E. EVALUATE Read the descriptions of things mentioned in the conversation. Is the effect of each one on our lives positive, negative, or both? What's your opinion? Add the letter for each item to one section of the Venn diagram.

a. a GPS that gives spoken directions to drivers

b. devices that answer your questions out loud

c. devices that children play games with and talk to

d. digital assistants that perform tasks around the home

e. devices that seem to act independently, such as talking by themselves

f. digital voices that make people feel less lonely

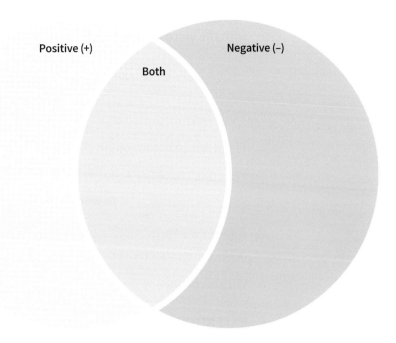

Positive (+)   Both   Negative (−)

F. INTERPRET Compare answers with a partner. Are your opinions similar or different? Give reasons for your opinions.

WORK WITH THE VIDEO

A. PREVIEW What was life like in your country 100 years ago? How was it different from life today?

VIDEO VOCABULARY

heat (v.) to become or to make something hot or warm

candle (n.) a stick of solid wax with a string through the middle, which you can burn to give light

iQ RESOURCES Go online to watch the video about life in Wales in 1927.
Resources > Video > Unit 4 > Unit Video

B. APPLY Watch the video two or three times. Then complete the sentences with the words in the box.

buy	cars	computers	electricity	kitchen	make	walk

1. There is no _____ or gas. There is only a fire in the kitchen.

2. There are no bathrooms in the house. They wash in the _____.

3. They don't have _____, and there is no bus. The men have to _____ to work.

4. It's not easy to _____ things, so people _____ many things themselves.

5. With no phones or _____, they have to make their own music.

C. EXTEND Watch the video again. Discuss the questions.

1. Do you think the participants in this program found this life easy or difficult? Why or why not?

2. What did the participants learn from the experiment?

 # SAY WHAT YOU THINK

SYNTHESIZE Think about the unit video, Listening 1, and Listening 2 as you discuss the questions.

1. Think about one new electronic device that you use frequently. Did this device change your life or your relationships? If so, how? If not, why not?

2. How dependent are you on electronic devices or other modern technology, such as cars or washing machines? Do you know how to manage without them?

3. Would you like to spend two or three months living without any modern technology? Why or why not?

Finding new words in a **dictionary** can be difficult. Sometimes you hear the word, but you don't see it. You may not know how to spell it. This can make it difficult to look up words. Try these ideas to help you.

- Sound out the word and write it down as you say it.

- Think about other spellings of the sounds. For example, think of the word *character*. The sound /k/ can be written as *k*, *c*, *ch*, or *qu*.

- Watch out for double letters. For example, you won't find *occasion* under words beginning with *oca*.

- If you can guess the meaning of the word, look up a synonym in the dictionary. You may find the word in the definition.

- If you have a computer, type the word as you hear it and then use the spell-check function. The computer may correct it for you.

Note: Some words have "silent letters." For example, the *k* in *know* and the *l* in *walk* are both silent.

 A. VOCABULARY Listen to the sentences. At the end of each sentence, the speaker is going to repeat one word from the sentence. Guess the spelling of each word. Then try to look up each one in your dictionary. Use one or more of the ideas from the Vocabulary Skill box.

TIP FOR SUCCESS

With online dictionaries and indexes, it is no longer necessary to know how to use alphabetical order to find things. However, this is still a useful skill. Take some time to learn the rules for alphabetical order in order to find items in a print dictionary or index.

	My guess	Correct spelling
1.		
2.		
3.		
4.		
5.		

B. DISCUSS Work with a partner. Compare your answers in Activity A. Then discuss the questions.

1. Which words were hard to find in the dictionary? Why?

2. Were there any words you did not find? If so, which ones?

3. Which ideas did you use to look for the words in Activity A? Which ideas do you think you are going to use in the future?

iQ PRACTICE Go online for more practice using the dictionary.
Practice > *Unit 4* > *Activity 10*

SPEAKING

OBJECTIVE ▶

At the end of this unit, you are going to take part in a panel discussion about the effects of social media on society. After the discussion, your classmates may ask you to clarify some of your statements or ideas. After you listen to your classmates' discussions, ask questions to clarify things you don't understand.

GRAMMAR Comparatives

We use **comparatives** to talk about the differences between two things. Comparatives often use *than* to connect the two things being compared. Comparatives can be either positive or negative.

To make a **positive comparative,** follow the rules below for one-syllable adjectives. For two-syllable words, use *more* before the adjective or adverb.

> Our lives are becoming **more public than** they were in the past.
> Online arguments are often **angrier than** face-to-face ones.
> Jon will get the message **more quickly** if you send it to his phone.

For **negative comparatives,** use *less* before the adjective or adverb.

> Our lives are becoming **less private**.
> Many people think online discussions are **less respectful than** face-to-face discussions.

These are the basic rules for forming comparative adjectives.

Rule	Adjective	Comparative
Add -*er* to one-syllable adjectives.	cheap	cheap**er**
Delete final -*e* before adding -*er*.	close	clos**er**
Some two-syllable adjectives take -*er*.	quiet	quiet**er**
Change final *y* to *i* before adding -*er*.	easy	easi**er**
Double the final consonant when the word ends with a single vowel and a consonant. Then add -*er*.	big	bigg**er**
Use *more* or *less* with adjectives that have two or more syllables.	creative	**more** creative **less** creative
Some adjectives have irregular comparative forms.	good bad	**better** **worse**

iQ RESOURCES Go online to watch the Grammar Skill Video.
Resources > Video > Unit 4 > Grammar Skill Video

A. APPLY Complete each sentence with a positive (+) or negative (–) comparative. Use the adjective or adverb in parentheses.

1 Studies have shown that teens who spend a lot of time on social media are _____ (lonely +) than teens who spend less time.

2. Using social media makes it _____ (easy +) to stay in touch with friends.

3. Now that I'm using the GPS, I get lost _____ (often –) than I used to.

4. After interacting with digital voices, some people felt _____ (lonely –) than before.

5. I'm becoming _____ (dependent +) on my smartphone every day.

6. Voice-activated devices are becoming _____ (common +) in our homes.

B. CREATE Complete each sentence with a comparative that expresses your opinion. Use the adjective in parentheses. Then discuss with a partner.

1. Sending a birthday card to someone online is _____ (meaningful) than sending a card in the mail.

2. Face-to-face conversations are _____ (interesting) than online conversations.

3. I sometimes think that my smartphone is _____ (intelligent) than I am.

4. Protecting my privacy online is _____ (important) to me than having a lot of online friends.

iQ PRACTICE Go online for more practice with comparatives.
Practice › Unit 4 › Activity 11

iQ PRACTICE Go online for the Grammar Expansion: order of adjectives.
Practice › Unit 4 › Activity 12

PRONUNCIATION Linking between consonant sounds

Sometimes one word ends and the following word begins with the same consonant sound. In this case, speakers often hold the first sound and **link** it to the next. They don't repeat the consonant sound. Knowing this will improve your comprehension and help you to speak more easily and fluently.

    We turn everything off and do things like play games.
    How does technology affect our relationships?

Note: When a word ends in silent *e*, the sound of the last consonant is still linked to the next word.

    I have very good relationships with my online friends.

A. IDENTIFY Listen to the sentences. Mark the link between consonants in each sentence. Then listen again and repeat.

1. Perhaps you should stop putting so much personal information online.

2. I read an online newspaper every morning.

3. He's putting up his website tomorrow.

4. Could you please take care of that for me?

5. In Dunbar's study, the average number of online friends was 150.

B. ANALYZE Work with a partner. Mark the links between consonants in each sentence. Then practice saying the sentences.

1. Don't delete too much information.

2. I think that *Are You Really My Friend?* is a great title for Tanja Hollander's book.

3. Let me make just one quick comment about that.

4. I have some more statistics about the number of users.

5. She received nine new friend requests yesterday.

iQ PRACTICE Go online for more practice with links between consonant sounds. *Practice ▸ Unit 4 ▸ Activity 13*

SPEAKING SKILL Asking for and giving clarification

Ask for **clarification** when you don't understand something.

Sometimes you can ask for clarification by repeating something the speaker has said and using question intonation. In Listening 2, Aran is surprised when Leo says his friends disconnected their device. He repeats the phrase with question intonation. Then Leo explains.

> **Aran:** What did they do?
> **Leo:** They disconnected it.
> **Aran:** Disconnected it?
> **Leo:** Yes, completely.

You can also use questions like these to ask for clarification.

> Could you explain . . . ?
> What do you mean? / Do you mean . . . ?
> What does _____ mean?
> What's a/an _____ ?

Use phrases like these to give clarification.

> What I mean is . . .
> What I'm saying is . . .
> That's right.
> That's not what I meant.
> Let me explain.

A. IDENTIFY Work with a partner. Read the excerpts from Listening 2. Underline the phrases the speakers use to ask for and give clarification.

1. **Leo:** Do you mean because people like me are beginning to interact with them as if they were real humans?

   Aran: That's right. It's almost as if the machines are becoming our friends.

2. **Aran:** In a way, it's nice to have all of these "smart" devices that can do things for us, but I think we need to be careful about how we use them.

   Leo: Be careful? What do you mean?

   Aran: What I'm saying is that we shouldn't become too dependent on these things.

B. CREATE Work in a small group. Follow these steps.

1. Choose a topic from the box or use your own idea.

   - Something I enjoy doing online
   - Something I prefer to do in person
   - An interesting website I recently visited
   - Why I want/don't want a digital assistant

2. Make some notes about your topic.

3. Speak to the group for one minute about your topic. When a listener asks for clarification, explain your idea again.

4. Listen to the other members of the group. When you don't understand something, ask for clarification.

iQ PRACTICE Go online for more practice with asking for and giving clarification. *Practice › Unit 4 › Activity 14*

UNIT ASSIGNMENT   **Have a panel discussion about social media**

OBJECTIVE ▶

In this section, you are going to work in a group to have a panel discussion about social media. As you prepare for your discussion, think about the Unit Question, "How does technology affect our relationships?" Use information from Listening 1, Listening 2, the unit video, and your work in this unit to support your presentation. Refer to the Self-Assessment checklist on page 88.

CONSIDER THE IDEAS

 INVESTIGATE Listen to the speaker introduce your panel discussion about social media and society. What are the three topics the speaker mentions? Write them below. Then think of one more possible topic of your own.

Topic 1: _____

Topic 2: _____

Topic 3: _____

Topic 4: _____

PREPARE AND SPEAK

A. GATHER IDEAS Work in a small group.

1. Discuss the question "Are social media sites good or bad for society?" Use the topics from Consider the Ideas as a guide, including one additional topic based on suggestions in Activity B. List as many pros (arguments for) and cons (arguments against) for each topic as you can.

TIP FOR SUCCESS

Brainstorming is a way of producing ideas by holding an informal group discussion.

2. Don't say "no" to any ideas yet. This is a process known as *brainstorming*. Take notes. Use symbols and abbreviations in order to write more quickly.

B. ORGANIZE IDEAS With your group, review notes from Activity A.

1. Choose the best ideas to create a chart like the one below, with a *Topic* column and columns for pros and cons.

Topic	Pros	Cons
Business		

2. Try to have an equal number of pros and cons. Use comparative forms whenever possible.

3. Organize the discussion. Make sure that each member of the group has a part.

C. SPEAK Practice your panel discussion. Then present the discussion to the class (or to another group). Refer to the Self-Assessment checklist below before you begin. After your discussion, invite classmates to ask questions about anything they didn't understand. Clarify and explain.

iQ PRACTICE Go online for your alternate Unit Assignment.
Practice > Unit 4 > Activity 15

CHECK AND REFLECT

A. CHECK Think about the Unit Assignment as you complete the Self-Assessment checklist.

SELF-ASSESSMENT	Yes	No
I was able to speak easily about the topic.	☐	☐
I used symbols and abbreviations in my notes.	☐	☐
My group or class understood me.	☐	☐
I used positive and negative comparatives correctly.	☐	☐
I used vocabulary from the unit.	☐	☐
I asked for and gave clarification.	☐	☐
I used links between consonant sounds.	☐	☐

B. REFLECT Discuss these questions with a partner or group.

1. What is something new you learned in this unit?

2. Look back at the Unit Question—How does technology affect our relationships? Is your answer different now than when you started this unit? If yes, how is it different? Why?

iQ PRACTICE Go to the online discussion board to discuss the questions.
Practice > Unit 4 > Activity 16

TRACK YOUR SUCCESS

iQ PRACTICE Go online to check the words and phrases you have learned in this unit. *Practice > Unit 4 > Activity 17*

Check (✓) the skills and strategies you learned. If you need more work on a skill, refer to the page(s) in parentheses.

NOTE-TAKING	☐ I can use symbols and abbreviations to take notes. (p. 70)
CRITICAL THINKING	☐ I can use my curiosity. (p. 74)
LISTENING	☐ I can listen for specific information. (p. 75)
VOCABULARY	☐ I can use the dictionary to find new words. (p. 81)
GRAMMAR	☐ I can use comparatives. (p. 82)
PRONUNCIATION	☐ I can link consonant sounds. (p. 84)
SPEAKING	☐ I can ask for and give clarification. (p. 85)

OBJECTIVE ▶ ☐ I can gather information and ideas to make a presentation about the effects of social media on society.

VOCABULARY LIST AND CEFR CORRELATION

🔑 The **Oxford 3000**™ is a list of the 3,000 core words that every learner of English needs to know. The words have been chosen based on their frequency in the Oxford English Corpus and relevance to learners of English. Every word is aligned to the CEFR, guiding learners on the words they should know at the A1–B2 level.

OPAL The **Oxford Phrasal Academic Lexicon** is an essential guide to the most important words and phrases to know for academic English. The word lists are based on the Oxford Corpus of Academic English and the British Academic Spoken English corpus.

The **Common European Framework of Reference for Language (CEFR)** provides a basic description of what language learners have to do to use language effectively. The system contains 6 reference levels: A1, A2, B1, B2, C1, C2.

UNIT 1

advertise *(v.)* 🔑 A2
affordable *(adj.)* B2
brake *(n.)*
buck the trend *(v. phr.)*
chat *(v.)* 🔑 A2
decline *(v.)* 🔑 OPAL B2
enormous *(adj.)* 🔑 A2
essential *(adj.)* 🔑 OPAL B1
failure *(n.)* 🔑 OPAL B2
get the point *(v. phr.)*
postage *(n.)*
potential *(adj.)* 🔑 OPAL B2
realize *(v.)* 🔑 A2
reasonable *(adj.)* 🔑 OPAL B2
wealthy *(adj.)* 🔑 B2
wheel *(n.)* 🔑 A2

UNIT 2

beautiful *(adj.)* 🔑 A1
blend in *(v. phr.)*
brilliant *(adj.)* 🔑 A2
hide *(v.)* 🔑 A2
insect *(n.)* 🔑 A2
match *(v.)* 🔑 B1
peaceful *(adj.)* 🔑 B1

poison *(n.)* 🔑 B1
predator *(n.)* C1
pride *(n.)* B2
shape *(n.)* 🔑 OPAL A2
skin *(n.)* 🔑 A2
solid *(adj.)* 🔑 B1
straight *(adj.)* 🔑 A2
survive *(v.)* 🔑 B1
warning *(n.)* 🔑 B1
wing *(n.)* 🔑 B1

UNIT 3

admit *(v.)* 🔑 B1
attentive *(adj.)*
behavior *(n.)* 🔑 OPAL A2
courteous *(adj.)*
courtesy *(n.)* C1
deal with *(v. phr.)* A2
etiquette *(n.)*
improve *(v.)* 🔑 OPAL A1
increase *(n.)* 🔑 OPAL A2
influence *(n.)* 🔑 OPAL B1
manners *(n.)* 🔑 A2
polite *(adj.)* 🔑 A2
principal *(n.)* B2
respect *(n.)* 🔑 OPAL B1

rude *(adj.)* 🔑 A2
scream *(v.)* 🔑 B2
shout out *(v. phr.)*
society *(n.)* 🔑 OPAL A2
valuable *(adj.)* 🔑 OPAL B1
violence *(n.)* 🔑 OPAL B2

UNIT 4

common *(adj.)* 🔑 OPAL A1
dependent on *(adj. phr.)* OPAL B2
digital *(adj.)* OPAL 🔑 A2
disconnect *(v.)*
face-to-face *(adj. phr. / adv. phr.)*
find *(v.)* OPAL 🔑 B1
forever *(adv.)* 🔑 B2
friendship *(n.)* 🔑 B1
headline *(n.)* 🔑 B1
meaningful *(adj.)* OPAL C1
post *(v.)* 🔑 A1
privacy *(n.)* 🔑 B2
relationship *(n.)* 🔑 OPAL A2
scary *(adj.)* 🔑 A2
silly *(adj.)* 🔑 B1
strange *(adj.)* 🔑 A2

UNIT 5

ancestor *(n.)* B2
appearance *(n.)* 🔑 A2
coincidence *(n.)* B2
cousin *(n.)* 🔑 A1
database *(n.)* B2
get along *(v. phr.)*
identity *(n.)* 🔑 OPAL B1
inherit *(v.)* B2
input *(n.)* OPAL B2
participant *(n.)* 🔑 OPAL B2
record *(n.)* 🔑 OPAL A2
search *(v.)* 🔑 A2
separate *(adj.)* 🔑 OPAL A2
slave *(n.)* 🔑 B2
tendency *(n.)* OPAL B2
twin *(n.)* 🔑 A2

UNIT 6

apply *(v.)* 🔑 OPAL B2
benefit *(n.)* 🔑 OPAL A2
coach *(n.)* 🔑 A2
competitive *(adj.)* 🔑 B1
developer *(n.)*
disappointment *(n.)* B2
entertainment *(n.)* 🔑 B1
lose *(v.)* 🔑 A1

object *(n.)* 🔑 OPAL B2
positive *(adj.)* 🔑 OPAL A1
pressure *(n.)* 🔑 OPAL B1
react *(v.)* 🔑 OPAL A2
stress *(n.)* 🔑 OPAL A2
tournament *(n.)* B2
useful *(adj.)* 🔑 OPAL A1
wonderful *(adj.)* 🔑 A1

UNIT 7

attack *(v.)* 🔑 OPAL A2
earthquake *(n.)* 🔑 B1
elevator *(n.)*
fascinating *(adj.)* 🔑 B1
freezing *(adj.)*
height *(n.)* 🔑 A2
neighborhood *(n.)* 🔑 B1
permanent *(adj.)* 🔑 B2
process *(v.)* 🔑 OPAL B2
remain *(v.)* 🔑 B1
resident *(n.)* 🔑 OPAL B2
response *(n.)* 🔑 OPAL A2
shake *(v.)* 🔑 A2
suburb *(n.)* B2
suitable *(adj.)* 🔑 OPAL B1
threat *(n.)* 🔑 OPAL B2

UNIT 8

agriculture *(n.)* B2
allergy *(n.)*
automatically *(adv.)* B2
bacteria *(n.)* 🔑 B2
climate *(n.)* 🔑 OPAL A2
consequence *(n.)* 🔑 OPAL B1
defense *(n.)* 🔑 B2
demand *(n.)* 🔑 OPAL B2
digest *(v.)*
dirt *(n.)* 🔑 B1
disease *(n.)* 🔑 A2
germs *(n.)*
grow *(v.)* 🔑 OPAL A1
lack of *(n. phr.)*
old-fashioned *(adj.)* 🔑 B1
prevent *(v.)* 🔑 OPAL A2
sensible *(adj.)* 🔑 B1
shortage *(n.)* B2
supply *(n.)* 🔑 OPAL B1

An impact study was undertaken to understand the perceived impact of *Q: Skills for Success* on improving the metacognitive skills students need for academic study. The research was conducted in October and November 2018. 115 teachers responded.

The Oxford Impact Framework is a systematic approach to evaluating the impact of Oxford University Press products and services. It was developed through a unique collaboration with the National Foundation for Educational Research (NFER) and is supported by the Oxford University Department of Education.

OXFORD IMPACT FRAMEWORK
EVALUATING EDUCATIONAL PRODUCTS AND SERVICES FROM OXFORD UNIVERSITY PRESS

CREATED WITH

Evidence for
Excellence in
Education

SUPPORTED BY

Department of Education
University of Oxford

Oxford University Press is the world's authority on the English language.

As part of the University of Oxford, we are committed to furthering English language learning worldwide.

We continuously bring together our experience, expertise and research to create resources such as this one, helping millions of learners of English to achieve their potential.

OXFORD
UNIVERSITY PRESS

THIRD EDITION

Q: Skills for Success
Think critically. Succeed academically.

90% of teachers who took part in an Oxford Impact study believe that *Q: Skills for Success* has improved the skills their students need for academic study.

The Third Edition builds on its question-centered approach with even more critical thinking, up-to-date topics, and a completely new assessment for learning program.

Enhanced critical thinking
New activities, strategies, and author-voiced videos develop students' critical thinking in every unit.

New topics chosen by teachers
Engaging themes like science, psychology, and technology inspire learning.

Clear learning outcomes
Students can evaluate their progress, reflect on their learning, and identify areas for improvement.

iQ Online Practice
www.iQ3eonlinepractice.com

Students can get extra skills practice, access audio and video, and check their progress. Log in on a computer, tablet, or mobile device.

For Students
- Student Book with iQ Online Practice
- Split Student Book with iQ Online Practice
- Also available in e-book format at www.oxfordlearnersbookshelf.com

For Teachers
- Teacher's Access Code Card provides access to iQ Online Practice, Classroom Presentation Tool, and all teacher resources, including tests and teaching notes
- Class Audio CDs

CEFR
B1
A2
A1

ISBN 978-0-19-490490-2

9 780194 904902

OXFORD

THIRD EDITION

INTRO A

OXFORD IMPACT
EVALUATED

Skills for Success
LISTENING AND SPEAKING

Kevin McClure | Mari Vargo

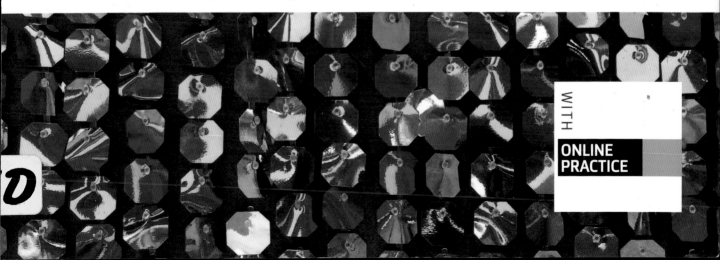

WITH
ONLINE
PRACTICE

Q: Skills for Success
THIRD EDITION

Important: Keep this code safe. Before you use your code, speak to your teacher.

How to access iQ Third Edition Online Practice

Note to Teachers: Please contact your sales representative for a Teacher Access Code.

❶ Go to www.iQ3eonlinepractice.com

❷ Choose Register to create your Oxford ID.

OR

Registered for iQ Third Edition Online Practice? Sign in and choose Add a level.

❸ Follow the instructions. Enter your access code.

You can only use your code once.

Your access code

S-392-467-4479

NEED HELP? Go to www.oup.com/elt/

Need more help? Email Customer Support at eltsupport@oup.com